Automotive Electrical & Electronics Concepts

Dr. P. Thangavel,
Professor,
Department of Mechanical Engineering
Erode Sengunthar Engineering College.
Thudupathi,
Perundurai,
Erode-638057

Dr.M.Vijay Anand
Professor
Department of Mechanical Engineering,
Erode Sengunthar Engineering College,
Perundurai,
Erode - 638057

Mr.M.Makeshkumar
Assistant Professor,
Department of Mechanical Engineering
Erode Sengunthar Engineering College.
Thudupathi.
Perundurai,
Erode-638057

AUTOMOTIVE ELECTRICAL AND ELECTRONICS   L T P C

                                            3 0 0 3

OBJECTIVE

☐ To impart knowledge to the students in the principles of operation and constructional details of various Automotive Electrical and Electronic Systems like Batteries, Starting System, Charging System, Ignition System, Lighting System and Dash – Board Instruments.

UNIT I   **TYPES OF BATTERIES**   9

Principle and construction of Lead Acid Battery, Nickel – Cadmium Battery, Nickel Metal, Hybrid Battery, Sodium Sulphur Battery and Aluminium Air Battery, Characteristics of Battery, Battery Rating, Capacity and Efficiency, Various Tests on Battery, Battery–Charging Techniques, .Maintenance of batteries.

UNIT II   **ELECTRICAL COMPONENTS**   9

Requirements of Starter Motor, Starter Motor types , construction and characteristics, Starter drive mechanisms, Starter Switches and Solenoids, Charging system components, Generators and Alternators ,types, construction and Characteristics . Voltage and Current Regulation, Cut –out relays and regulators, Charging circuits for D.C. Generator, A.C. Single Phase and Three – Phase Alternators.

UNIT III   **IGNITION SYSTEMS**   9

Battery Coil and Magneto–Ignition System, Circuit details and Components of Battery Coil and Magneto–Ignition System, Centrifugal and Vacuum Advance Mechanisms, Spark Plugs, Constructional details and Types.

UNIT IV   **ELECTRICAL AND ELECTRONIC IGNITION SYSYTEMS**   9

Electronically–Assisted and Full Electronic Ignition System, Non–Contact–type Ignition Triggering devices, Capacitive Discharge Ignition Distributor–less Ignition System, Digital Ignition System, Control Strategy of Electronic Ignition System.

UNIT V   **WIRING, LIGHTING AND OTHER INSTRUMENTS AND SENSORS**   9

Automotive Wiring, Insulated and Earth Return System, Positive and Negative Earth Systems, Head Lamp and Indicator Lamp Details, Anti–Dazzling and Dipper Details, Electrical and Electronic Fuel Lift Pumps, Theory and Constructional Details of Dash Board Instruments and their Sensors like Speedometer, Odometer, Fuel Level Indicator Oil Pressure and Coolant Temperature Indicators, Horns and Wiper Mechanisms, Automotive Wiring Circuits.

Lead-acid batteries

Construction

Even after well over 100 years of development and much promising research into other techniques of energy storage, the lead-acid battery is still the best choice for motor vehicle use. This is particularly so when cost and energy density are taken into account. Incremental changes over the years have made the sealed and maintenance-free battery now in common use very reliable and long lasting. This may not always appear to be the case to some end-users, but note that quality is often related to the price the customer pays. Many bottom-of-the-range cheap batteries, with a 12 month guarantee, will last for 13 months! The basic construction of a nominal 12 V leadacid battery consists of six cells connected in series. Each cell, producing about 2 V, is housed in an individual compartment within a polypropylene, or similar, case. Figure shows a cut-away battery showing the main component parts.

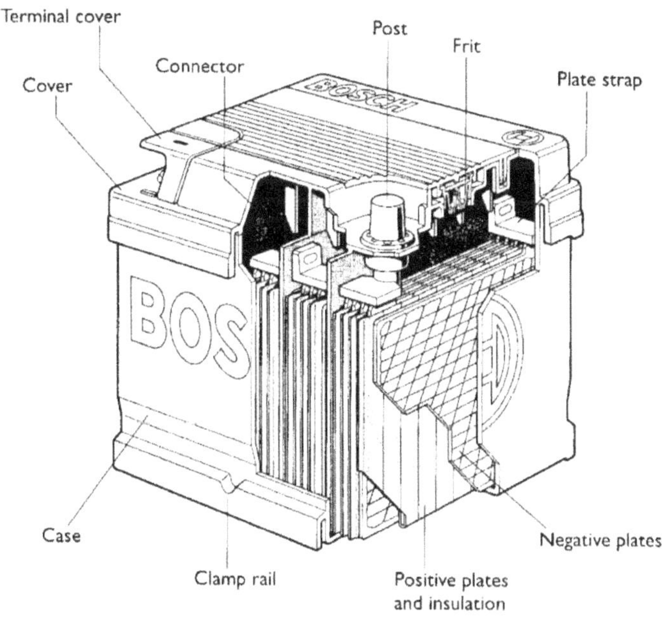

Lead Acid Battery

The active material is held in grids or baskets to form the positive and negative plates. Separators made from a microporous plastic insulate these plates from each other. The grids, connecting strips and the battery posts are made from a lead alloy. For many years this was lead antimony (PbSb) but this has now been largely replaced by lead calcium (PbCa). The newer materials cause less gassing of the electrolyte when the battery is fully charged. This has been one of the main reasons why sealed batteries became feasible, as water loss is considerably reduced. However, even modern batteries described as sealed do still have a small vent to stop the pressure build-up due to the very small amount of gassing. A further requirement of sealed batteries is accurate control of charging voltage.

Battery rating

In simple terms, the characteristics or rating of a particular battery are determined by how much current it can produce and how long it can sustain this current. The rate at which a battery can produce current is determined by the speed of the chemical reaction.

This in turn is determined by a number of factors:

- Surface area of the plates.
- Temperature.
- Electrolyte strength.
- Current demanded.

The actual current supplied therefore determines the overall capacity of a battery. The rating of a battery has to specify the current output and the time.

Ampere hour capacity

This is now seldom used but describes how much current the battery is able to supply for either 10 or 20 hours. The 20-hour figure is the most common. For example, a battery quoted as being 44 Ah (ampere-hour) will be able, if fully charged, to supply 2.2 A for 20 hours before being completely discharged (cell voltage above 1.75 V).

Reserve capacity

A system used now on all new batteries is reserve capacity. This is quoted as a time in minutes for which the battery will supply 25 A at 25 ° C to a final voltage of 1.75 V per cell. This is used to give an indication of how long the battery could run the car if the charging system was not working. Typically, a 44 Ah battery will have a reserve capacity of about 60 minutes.

Cold cranking amps

Batteries are given a rating to indicate performance at high current output and at low temperature. A typical value of 170 A means that the battery will supply this current for one minute at a temperature of _18 ° C, at which point the cell voltage will fall to 1.4 V (BS – British Standards).

Note that the overall output of a battery is much greater when spread over a longer time. As mentioned above, this is because the chemical reaction can only work at a certain speed. Figure 5.3 shows the above three discharge characteristics and how they can be compared.

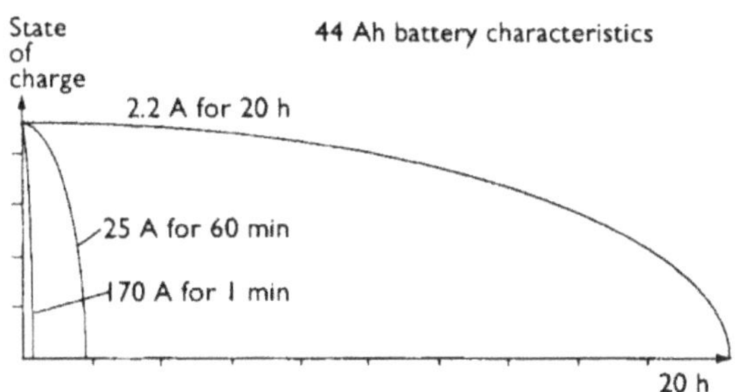

Battery discharge characteristics compared

Maintenance and charging

Maintenance

By far the majority of batteries now available are classed as 'maintenance free'. This implies that little attention is required during the life of the battery. Earlier batteries and some heavier types do, however, still require the electrolyte level to be checked and topped up periodically.

Battery posts are still a little prone to corrosion and hence the usual service of cleaning with hot water if appropriate and the application of petroleum jelly or proprietary terminal grease is still recommended. Ensuring that the battery case and, in particular, the top remains clean, will help to reduce the rate of self-discharge.

The state of charge of a battery is still very important and, in general, it is not advisable to allow the state of charge to fall below 70% for long periods as the sulphate on the plates can harden, making recharging difficult. If a battery is to be stored for a long period (more than a few weeks , then it must be recharged every so often to prevent it from becoming sulphated. Recommendations vary but a recharge every six weeks is a reasonable suggestion.

Battery Charging

The recharging recommendations of battery manufacturers vary slightly. The following methods, however, are reasonably compatible and should not cause any problems. The recharging process must 'put back' the same ampere-hour capacity as was used on discharge plus a bit more to allow for losses. It is therefore clear that the main question about charging is not how much, but at what rate.

The old recommendation was that the battery should be charged at a tenth of its ampere-hour capacity for about 10 hours or less. This is assuming that the ampere-hour capacity is quoted at the 20 hour rate, as a tenth of this figure will make allowance for the charge factor. This figure is still valid, But as ampere-hour capacity is not always used nowadays, a different method of deciding the rate is necessary. One way is to set a rate at 1/16 of the reserve capacity, again for up to 10 hours. The final suggestion is to set a charge rate at 1/40 of the cold start

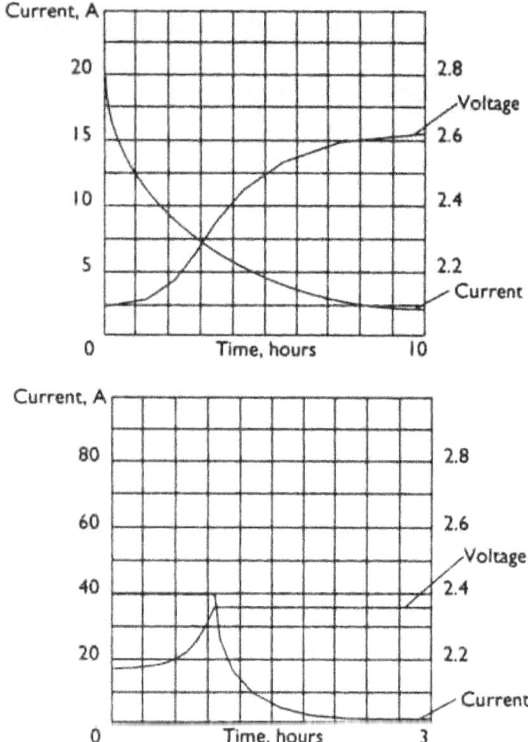

Two ways of charging a battery showing the relationship between charging voltage and charging current

Charging method   Notes

Charging method	Notes
Constant voltage	Will recharge any battery in 7 hours or less without any risk of overcharging (14.4 V maximum).
Constant current	Ideal charge rate can be estimated as: 1/10 of Ah capacity, 1/16 of reserve capacity or 1/40 of cold start current (charge time of 10–12 hours or pro rata original state).

Boost charging   At no more than five times the ideal rate, a battery can be brought up to about 70% of charge in about one hour.

Performance figure, also for up to 10 hours. Clearly, if a battery is already half charged, half the time is required to recharge to full capacity. The above suggested charge rates are to be recommended as the best way to prolong battery life. They do all, however, Imply a constant current charging source. A constant voltage charging system is often the best way to charge a battery. This implies that the charger, an alternator on a car for example, is held at a constant level and the state of charge in the battery will determine how much current will flow. This is often the fastest way to recharge a flat battery. The two ways of charging are represented in Figure. This shows the relationship between charging voltage and the charging current. If a constant voltage of less than 14.4 V is used then it is not possible to cause excessive gassing and this method is particularly appropriate for sealed batteries. Boost charging is a popular technique often applied in many workshops. It is not recommended as the best method but, if correctly administered and not repeated too often, is suitable for most batteries. The key to fast or boost charging is that the battery temperature should not exceed 43° C. With sealed batteries it is particularly important not to let the battery create excessive gas in order to prevent the build-up of pressure. A rate of about five times the 'normal' charge setting will bring the battery to 78–80% of its full capacity within approximately one hour. Table summarizes the charging techniques for a lead-acid battery. Figure shows a typical battery charger.

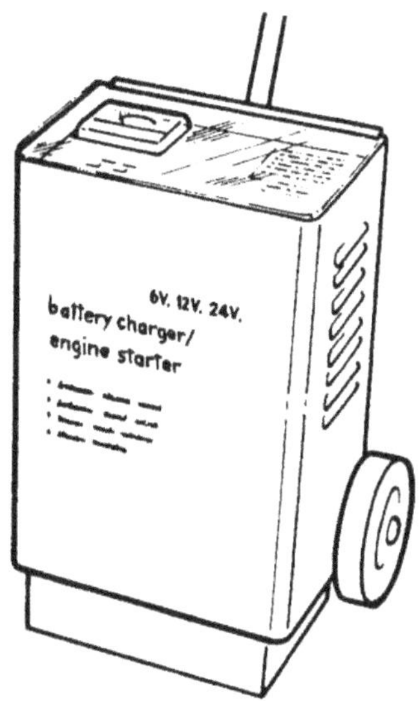

Battery Charger

Various Tests on Battery

For testing the state of charge of a non-sealed type of battery, a hydrometer can be used, as shown in Figure The hydrometer comprises a syringe that draws electrolyte from a cell, and a float that will float at a particular depth in the electrolyte according to its density. The density or specific gravity is then read from the graduated scale on the float. A fully charged cell should show 1.280, 1.200 when half charged and 1.130 if discharged.

Most vehicles are now fitted with maintenance free batteries and a hydrometer cannot be used to find the state of charge. This can only be determined. From the voltage of the battery, as given in Table. An accurate voltmeter is required for this test. A heavy-duty (HD) discharge tester as shown in Figure is an instrument consisting of a low-value resistor and a voltmeter connected to a pair of heavy test prods. The test prods are firmly pressed on to the battery terminals. The voltmeter reads the voltage of the battery on heavy discharge of 200–300 A. Assuming a battery to be in a fully charged condition, a serviceable battery should read about 10V for a period of about 10 s. A sharply falling battery voltage to below 3 V indicates an unserviceable cell. Note also if any cells are gassing, as this indicates a short circuit. A zero or extremely low reading can indicate an open circuit cell. When using the HD tester, the following precautions must be observed:

● Blow gently across the top of the battery to remove flammable gases.

● The test prods must be positively and firmly pressed into the lead terminals of the battery to minimize sparking.

● It should not be used while a battery is on charge.

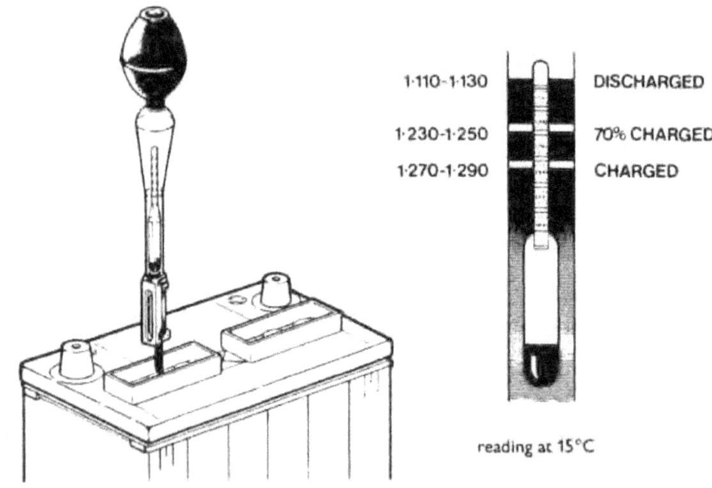

Hydrometer Test of a Battery

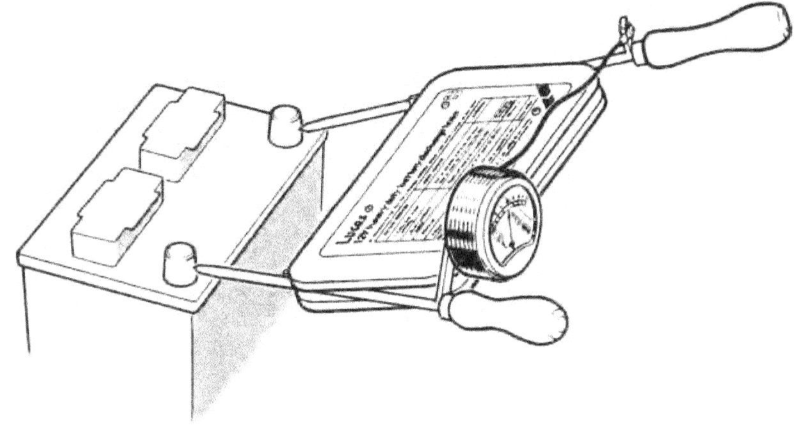

Heavy Duty Discharge Test

State of charge of a battery

Battery volts at 20 ° C	State of charge
12.0	Discharged (20% or less)
12.3	Half charged (50%)
12.7	Charged (100%)

SODIUM SULPHUR BATTERY

Much research is underway to improve on current battery technology in order to provide a greater energy density for electric vehicles. A potential major step forwards however the sodium sulphur battery, which has now reached production stage. Sodium-sulphur batteries have recently reached the production stage and, in common with the other types listed, have much potential; however, all types have specific drawbacks. For example, storing and carrying hydrogen is one problem of fuel cells.

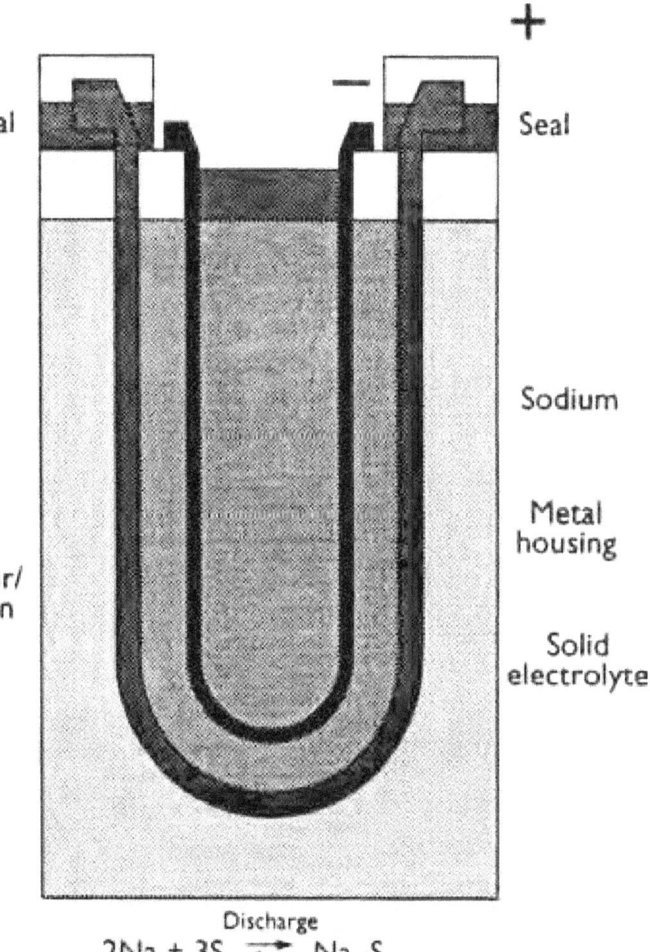

$$2Na + 3S \rightleftharpoons Na_2 S_3$$

The sodium-sulphur or NaS battery consists of a cathode of liquid sodium into which is placed a current collector. This is a solid electrode of β-alumina. A metal can that is in contact with the anode (a sulphur electrode) surrounds the whole assembly. The major problem with this system is that the running temperature needs to be 300–350 ° C. A heater rated at a few hundred watts forms part of the charging circuit. This maintains the battery temperature when the vehicle is not running. Battery temperature is maintained when in use due to $I^2 R$ losses in the battery.

Each cell of this battery is very small, using only about 15 g of sodium. This is a safety feature because, if the cell is damaged, the sulphur on the outside will cause the potentially dangerous sodium to be converted into polysulphides – which are comparatively harmless. Small cells also have the advantage that they can be distributed around the car. The capacity of each cell is about 10 Ah. These cells fail in an open circuit condition and hence this must be taken into account, as the whole string of cells used to create the required voltage would be rendered inoperative. The output voltage of each cell is about 2V. A problem still to be overcome is the casing material, which is prone to fail due to the very corrosive nature of the sodium. At present, an expensive chromized coating is used.

This type of battery, supplying an electric motor, is becoming a competitor to the internal combustion engine. The whole service and charging infrastructure needs to develop but looks promising. It is estimated that the cost of running an electric vehicle will be as little as 15% of the petrol version, which leaves room to absorb the extra cost of production.

Alkaline batteries (Nickel – Cadmium Battery)

Lead-acid batteries traditionally required a considerable amount of servicing to keep them in good condition, although this is not now the case with the advent of sealed and maintenance-free batteries.

However, when a battery is required to withstand a high rate of charge and discharge on a regular basis, or is left in a state of disuse for long periods, the lead-acid cell is not ideal. Alkaline cells on the other hand require minimum maintenance and are far better able to withstand electrical abuse such as heavy discharge and over-charging.

The disadvantages of alkaline batteries are that they are more bulky, have lower energy efficiency and are more expensive than a lead-acid equivalent. When the lifetime of the battery and servicing requirements are considered, the extra initial cost is worth it for some applications. Bus and coach companies and some large goods-vehicle operators have used alkaline batteries.

Alkaline batteries used for vehicle applications are generally the nickel-cadmium type, as the other main variety (nickel-iron) is less suited to vehicle use. The main components of the nickel-cadmium – or Nicad – cell for vehicle use are as follows:

_ positive plate – nickel hydrate (NiOOH);

_ negative plate – cadmium (Cd);

_ electrolyte – potassium hydroxide (KOH) and water (H2O).

The process of charging involves the oxygen moving from the negative plate to the positive plate, and the reverse when discharging. When fully charged, the negative plate becomes pure cadmium and the positive plate becomes nickel hydrate. A chemical equation to represent this reaction is given next but notes that this is simplifying a more complex reaction.

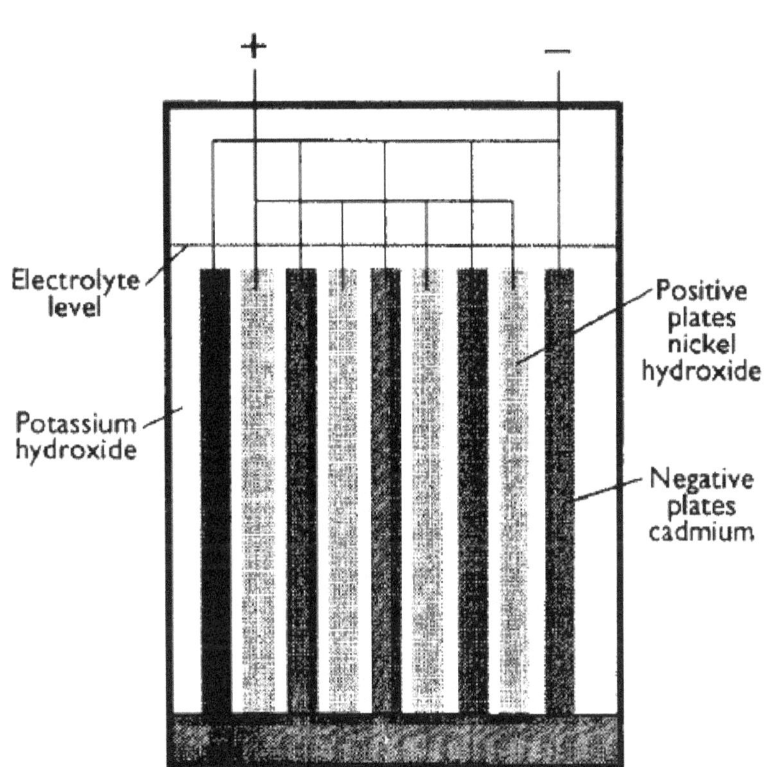

Figure 5.10 Simplified representation of a Nicad alkaline battery cell

$$2NiOOH + Cd + 2H_2O + KOH \leftrightarrow$$
$$2Ni(OH)_2 + CdO_2 + KOH$$

The $2H_2O$ is actually given off as hydrogen (H) and oxygen (O_2) as gassing takes place all the time during charge. It is this use of water by the cells that indicates they are operating, as will have been noted from the equation. The electrolyte does not change during the reaction. This means that a relative density reading will not indicate the state of charge. These batteries do not suffer from over-charging because once the cadmium oxide has changed to cadmium, no further reaction can take place. The cell voltage of a fully charged cell is 1.4V but this falls rapidly to 1.3 V as soon as discharge starts. The cell is discharged at a cell voltage of 1.1V.

ALUMINIUM–AIR BATTERY

Aluminium–air batteries or Al–air batteries produce electricity from the reaction of oxygen in the air with aluminium. They have one of the highest energy densities of all batteries, but they are not widely used because of problems with high anode cost and byproduct removal when using traditional electrolytes and this has restricted their use to mainly military applications. However, an electric vehicle with aluminium batteries has the potential for up to eight times the range of a lithium-ion battery with a significantly lower total weight.

Aluminium–air batteries are primary cells; i.e., non-rechargeable. Once the aluminium anode is consumed by its reaction with atmospheric oxygen at a cathode immersed in a water-based electrolyte to form hydrated aluminium oxide, the battery will no longer produce electricity. However, it is possible to mechanically recharge the battery with new aluminium anodes made from recycling the hydrated aluminium oxide. Such recycling would be essential if aluminium–air batteries are to be widely adopted.

Electrochemistry

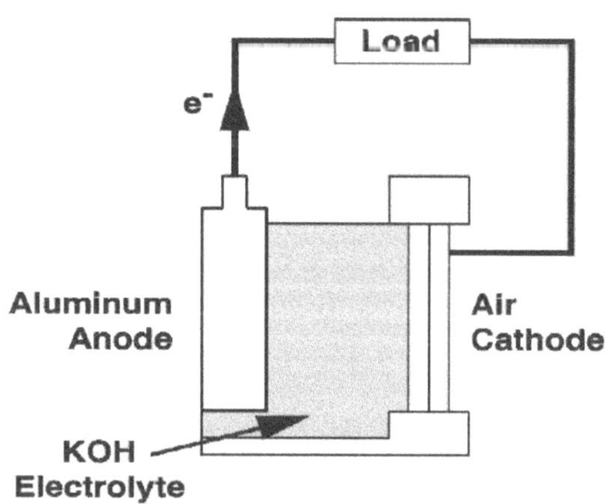

The anode oxidation half-reaction is

$$Al + 3OH^- \rightarrow Al(OH)_3 + 3e^- \quad -2.31\ V.$$

The cathode reduction half-reaction is

$$O_2 + 2H_2O + 4e^- \rightarrow 4OH^- +0.40 \text{ V}.$$

The total reaction is

$$4Al + 3O_2 + 6H_2O \rightarrow 4Al(OH)_3 + 2.71 \text{ V}.$$

About 1.2 volts potential difference is created by these reactions, and is achievable in practice when potassium hydroxide is used as the electrolyte. Saltwater electrolyte achieves approximately 0.7 volts per cell.

NICKEL–METAL HYDRIDE BATTERY

A nickel–metal hydride battery, abbreviated NiMH or Ni–MH, is a type of rechargeable battery. Its chemical reactions are somewhat similar to the largely obsolete nickel–cadmium cell (NiCd). NiMH use positive electrodes of nickel oxyhydroxide (NiOOH), like the NiCd, but the negative electrodes use a hydrogen-absorbing alloy instead of cadmium, being in essence a practical application of nickel–hydrogen battery chemistry. A NiMH battery can have two to three times the capacity of an equivalent size NiCd, and their energy density approaches that of a lithium-ion cell.

The typical specific energy for small NiMH cells is about 100 W·h/kg, and for larger NiMH cells about 75 W·h/kg (270 kJ/kg). This is significantly better than the typical 40–60 W·h/kg for NiCd, and similar to the 100–160 W·h/kg for lithium-ion batteries. NiMH has a volumetric energy density of about 300 W·h/L (1,080 MJ/m3), significantly better than NiCd at 50–150 W·h/L, and about the same as lithium-ion at 250–360 W·h/L.

NiMH batteries have replaced NiCd for many roles, notably small rechargeable batteries. NiMH batteries are very common for AA (penlight-size) batteries, which have nominal charge capacities (C) of 1.1–2.8 A·h at 1.2 V, measured at the rate that discharges the cell in five hours. Useful discharge capacity is a decreasing function of the discharge rate, but up to a rate of around 1×C (full discharge in one hour), it does not differ significantly from the nominal capacity. NiMH batteries normally operate at 1.2 V per cell, somewhat lower than conventional 1.5 V cells, but will operate most devices designed for that voltage.

Electrochemistry

The negative electrode reaction occurring in a NiMH cell is:

$$H_2O + M + e^- \rightleftharpoons OH^- + MH$$

The charge reaction is read left-to-right and the discharge reaction is read right-to-left.

On the positive electrode, nickel oxyhydroxide, NiO(OH), is formed:

$$Ni(OH)_2 + OH^- \rightleftharpoons NiO(OH) + H_2$$

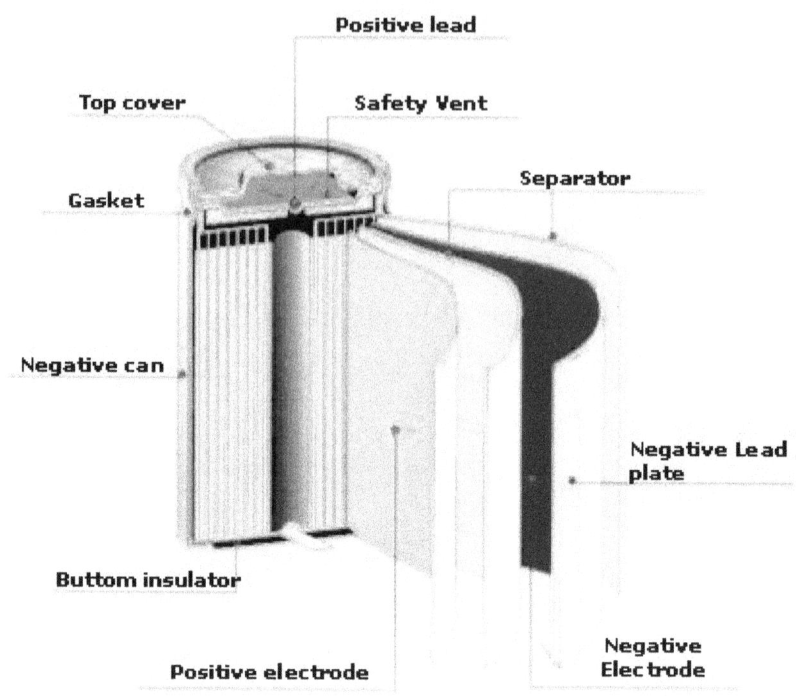

The "metal" M in the negative electrode of a NiMH cell is actually an intermetallic compound. Many different compounds have been developed for this application, but those in current use fall into two classes. The most common is AB_5 , where A is a rare earth mixture of lanthanum, cerium, neodymium, praseodymium and B is nickel, cobalt, manganese, and/or aluminium. Very few cells use higher-capacity negative electrode materials based on AB_2 compounds, where A is titanium and/or vanadium and B is zirconium or nickel, modified with chromium, cobalt, iron, and/or manganese, due to the reduced life performances. Any of these compounds serve the same role, reversibly forming a mixture of metal hydride compounds.

When overcharged at low rates, oxygen produced at the positive electrode passes through the separator and recombines at the surface of the negative. Hydrogen evolution is suppressed and the charging energy is converted to heat. This process allows NiMH cells to remain sealed in normal operation and to be maintenance-free.

NiMH cells have an alkaline electrolyte, usually potassium hydroxide. For separation hydrophilic polyolefin nonwovens are used.

Characteristics of Battery

Internal Resistance

- Temperature and state of charge affect the internal resistance of a battery.

- The internal resistance can also be used as an indicator of battery condition –the lower the figure, the better the condition.

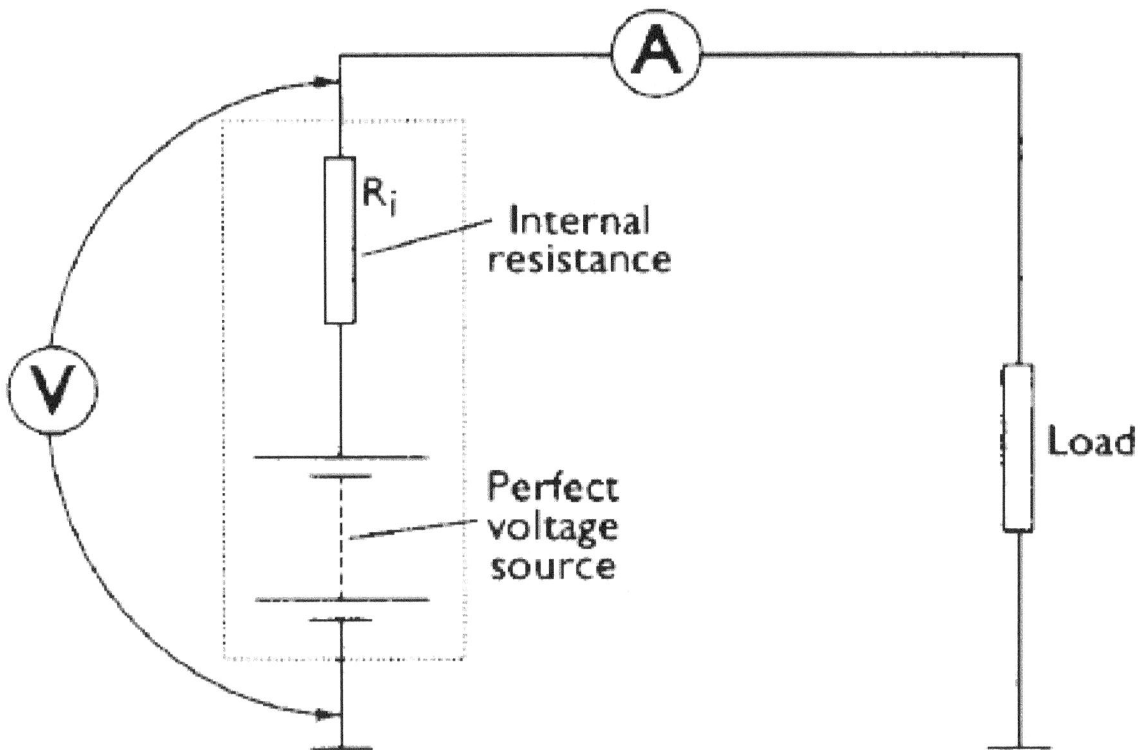

Efficiency

- The efficiency of a battery can be calculated in two ways, either as the ampere-hour efficiency or the power efficiency.

Ahr (or charge) efficiency

- In an ideal world a battery would return the entire charge put into it, in which case the amp hour efficiency is 100%. However, no battery does; its charging efficiency is less than 100%.

Energy efficiency

It is defined as the ratio of electrical energy supplied by a battery to the amount of electrical energy required to return it to the state before discharge.

Self-discharge

- All batteries suffer from self-discharge, which means that even without an external circuit the state of charge is reduced.

- The rate of discharge is of the order of 0.2–1% of the Ah capacity per day. This increases with temperature and the age of the battery.

- The chemical process

- Leakage current across top of the battery

Specific energy

- Specific energy is the amount of electrical energy stored for every kilogram of battery mass. It has units of *Wh.kg−1*

Energy density

- Energy density is the amount of electrical energy stored per cubic meter of battery volume. It normally has units of *Wh.m−3*

Specific power

- Specific power is the amount of power obtained per kilogram of battery. It is a highly variable and rather anomalous quantity, since the power given out by the battery depends far more upon the load connected to it than the battery itself.

Battery temperature, heating and cooling needs

- Although most batteries run at ambient temperature, some run at higher temperatures and need heating to start with and then cooling when in use.

- In others, battery performance drops off at low temperatures, which is undesirable, but this problem could be overcome by heating the battery.

Battery life and number of deep cycles

- Most rechargeable batteries will only undergo a few hundred deep cycles to 20% of the battery charge.

- However, the exact number depends on the battery type, and also on the details of the battery design, and on how the battery is used.

Unit-2

Electrical Components

Starter Motor types , construction and characteristics

Reducing electrical and mechanical stress at start-up, the starting current of an AC motor can vary from 3 to 7times the nominal current. This is because a large amount of energy is required to magnetise the motor enough to overcome the inertia the system has at standstill. The high current drawn from the network can cause problems such as voltage drop, high transients and, in some cases, uncontrolled shutdown. High starting current also causes great mechanical stress on the motor's rotor bars and windings, and can affect the driven equipment and the foundations. Several starting methods exist, all aiming to reduce these stresses.

The load, the motor and the supply network determine the most appropriate starting method. When selecting and dimensioning the starting equipment and any protective devices, the following factors must be taken into account:

–– The voltage drop in the supply network when starting the motor

–– The required load torque during start

–– The required starting time

Direct-on-line (DOL) start

Direct on line starting is suitable for stable supplies and mechanically stiff and well-dimensioned shaft systems. It is the simplest, cheapest and most common starting method. Starting equipment for small motors that do not start and stop frequently is simple, often consisting of a hand operated motor protection circuit breaker. Larger motors and motors that start and stop frequently, or have some kind of control system, normally use a direct-on-line starter which can consist of a contactor plus overload protection, such as a thermal relay.

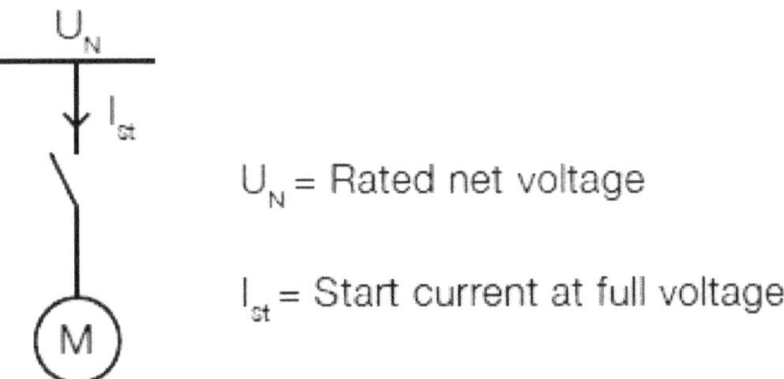

Star-Delta (Y/D) starting

Most low voltage motors can be connected to run at either 400 V with delta connection or at 690 V with star connection. This flexibility can also be used to start the motor with a lower voltage. Star/delta connection gives a low starting current of only about one-third of that during direct-on-line starting, although this also reduces the starting torque to about 25%.

The motor is started with Y-connection and accelerated as far as possible, then switched to D-connection. This method can only be used with induction motors delta connected for the supply voltage.

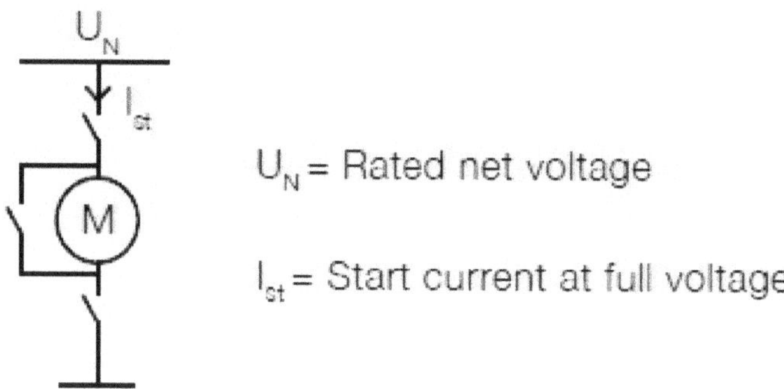

Reactor start

By connecting a coil with an iron core (a reactor) in series with the motor during start, the starting current is limited in proportion with the voltage. However, this also means a substantial (quadratic) reduction in the available starting torque.

The advantage of this method is its low cost in comparison with other methods.

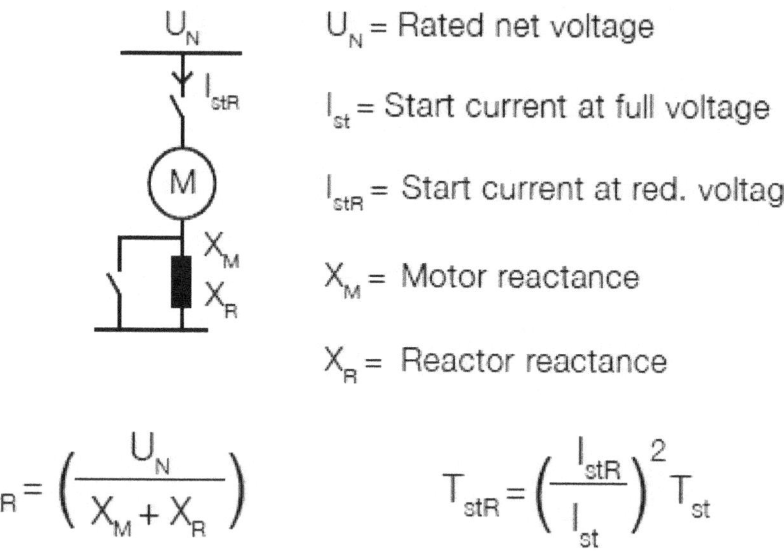

$$I_{stR} = \left(\frac{U_N}{X_M + X_R}\right) \qquad T_{stR} = \left(\frac{I_{stR}}{I_{st}}\right)^2 T_{st}$$

Auto transformer start

The effect of auto transformer start is similar to that of reactor start. Using a transformer to limit the voltage reduces the starting current and the torque, but less so than the reactor start. The method is more expensive than reactor start.

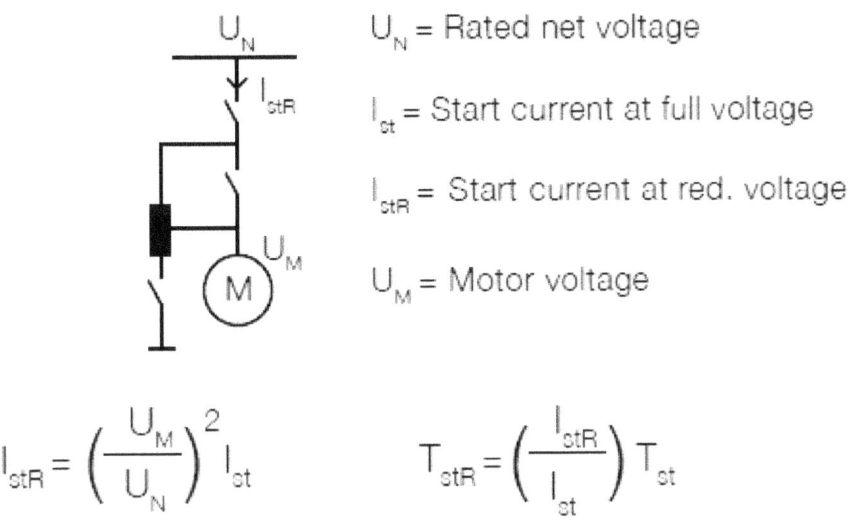

U_N = Rated net voltage

I_{st} = Start current at full voltage

I_{stR} = Start current at red. voltage

U_M = Motor voltage

$$I_{stR} = \left(\frac{U_M}{U_N}\right)^2 I_{st} \qquad T_{stR} = \left(\frac{I_{stR}}{I_{st}}\right) T_{st}$$

Capacitor start

By storing the power required for magnetisation in capacitor banks, it is possible to start with full starting torque without disturbing the network. To avoid over-compensation, the capacitor bank must be uncoupled after start-up. The disadvantages of this method are the high cost, and the large space requirement of the capacitor banks.

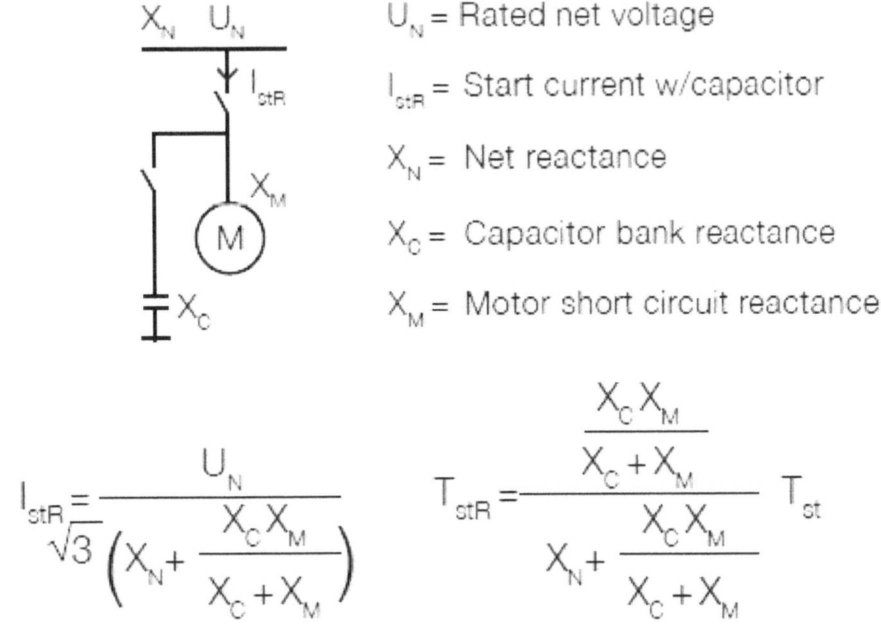

U_N = Rated net voltage

I_{stR} = Start current w/capacitor

X_N = Net reactance

X_C = Capacitor bank reactance

X_M = Motor short circuit reactance

$$I_{stR} = \frac{U_N}{\sqrt{3}\left(X_N + \dfrac{X_C X_M}{X_C + X_M}\right)} \qquad T_{stR} = \frac{\dfrac{X_C X_M}{X_C + X_M}}{X_N + \dfrac{X_C X_M}{X_C + X_M}} T_{st}$$

Soft starters

Soft starters are based on semiconductors, which, via a power circuit and a control circuit, initially reduces the motor voltage, resulting in lower motor torque. During the starting process, the soft starter progressively increases the motor voltage so that the motor becomes strong enough to accelerate the load to rated speed without causing torque or current peaks. Soft starters can also be used to control the stopping of a process. Soft starters are less costly than frequency converters but like frequency converters, they may inject harmonic currents into the grid, disrupting other processes.

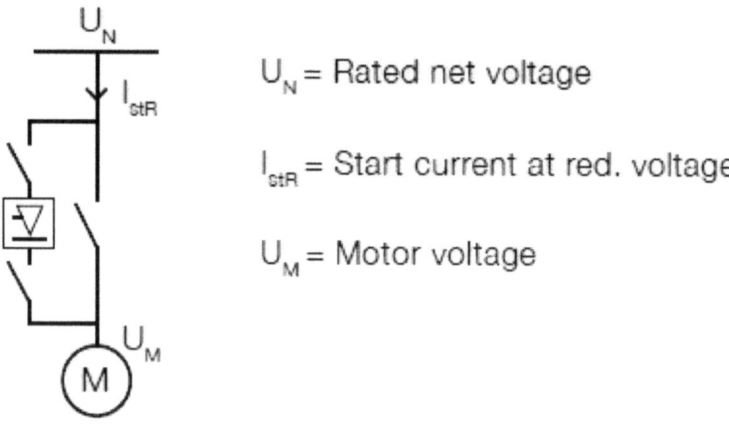

Frequency converter start

Although a frequency converter is designed for continuous feeding of motors, it can also be used for start-up only. The frequency converter enables low starting current because the motor can produce rated torque at rated current from zero to full speed. As the price of frequency converters continues to drop, they are increasingly being used in applications where soft starters would previously have been used. However in most cases they are still more expensive than soft starters, and like these, they inject harmonic currents into the network.

Rheostat starting

Rheostat starting can only be used with slip ring motors. On these motors, the resistance of the rotor circuits can be increased with an external resistor. This method is usually chosen when the supply net is weak and the required starting torque and moment of inertia are very high. By switching in the additional resistances in steps, normally 4 to 7 steps, the desired acceleration torque can be obtained. The normal DOL starting equipment also required.

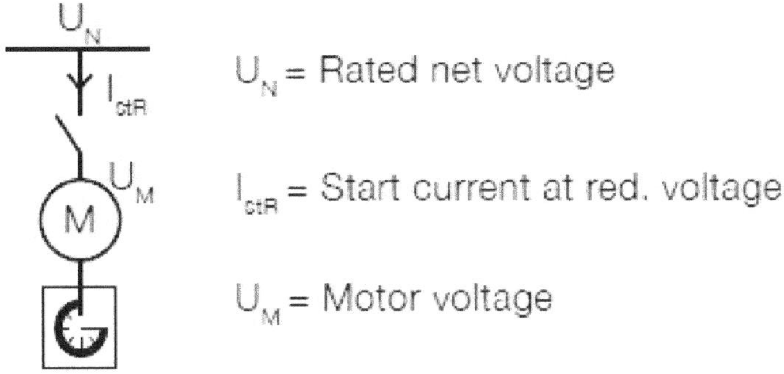

Requirements of Starter Motor

As a very general guide the stalled (locked) starter torque required per litre of engine capacity at the starting limit temperature is as shown in Table. A greater torque is required for engines with a lower number of cylinders due to the greater piston displacement per cylinder. This will determine the peak torque values. The other main factor is compression ratio.

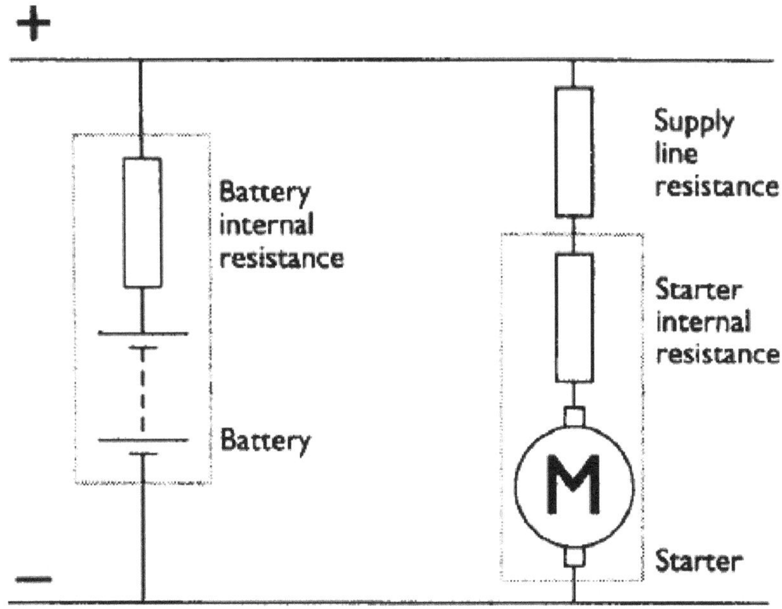

Equivalent circuit for a starter system

Torque required for various engine sizes

Engine cylinders	Torque per litre [Nm]
2	12.5
4	8.0
6	6.5
8	6.0
12	5.5

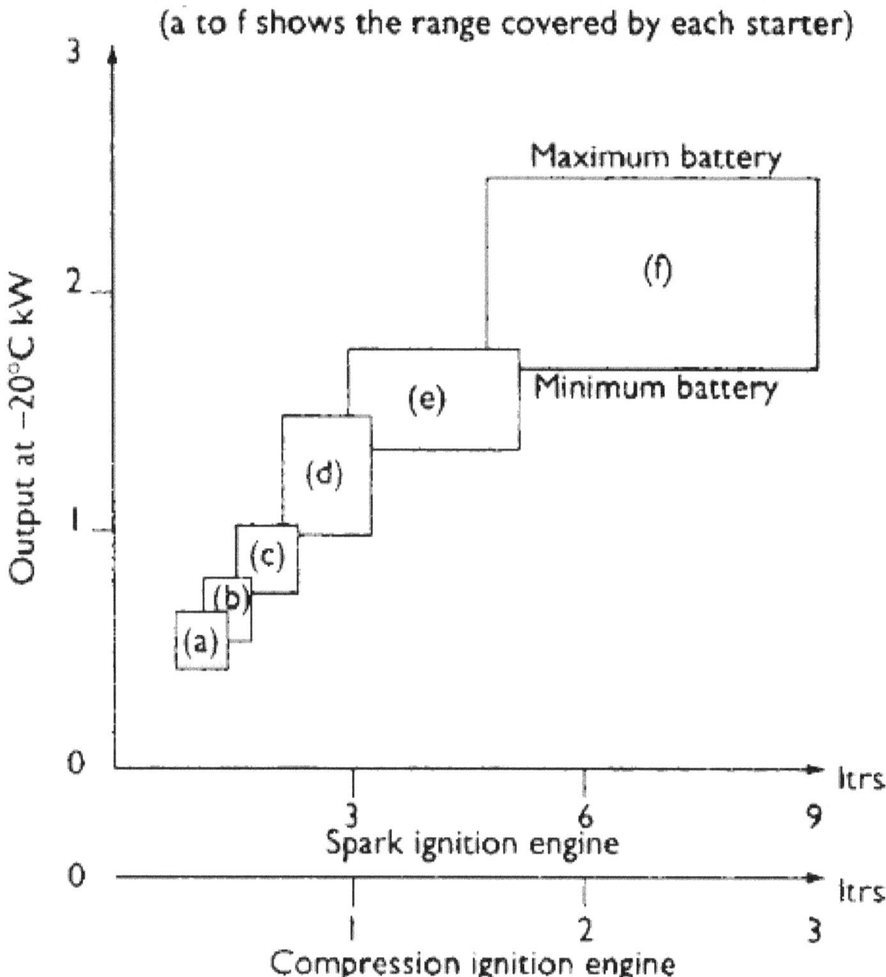

To illustrate the link between torque and power, we can assume that, under the worst conditions (_20 ° C), a four-cylinder 2-litre engine requires 480 Nm to overcome static friction and 160 Nm to maintain the minimum cranking speed of 100 rev/min. With a starter pinion-to-ring gear ratio of 10 : 1,the motor must therefore, be able to produce a maximum stalled torque of 48 Nm and a driving torque of 16 Nm. This is working on the assumption that stalled torque is generally three to four times the cranking torque.

Starter drive mechanisms

Inertia starters

In all standard motor vehicle applications it is necessary to connect the starter to the engine ring gear only during the starting phase. If the connection remained permanent, the excessive speed at which the starter would be driven by the engine would destroy the motor almost immediately. The inertia type of starter motor has been the technique used for over 80 years, but is now becoming redundant. The starter shown in Figure shows the Lucas M35J type. It is a four-pole, four-brush machine and was used on small to medium-sized petrol engined vehicles. It is capable of producing 9.6 Nm with a current draw of 350 A. The M35J uses a face-type commutator and axially aligned brush gear. The fields are wave wound and are earthed to the starter yoke. The starter engages with the flywheel ring gear by means of a small pinion. The toothed pinion and a sleeve splined on to the armature shaft are threaded such that when the starter is operated, via a remote relay, the armature will cause the sleeve to rotate inside the pinion. The pinion remains still due to its inertia and, because of the screwed sleeve rotating inside it, the pinion is moved to mesh with the ring gear.

When the engine fires and runs under its own power, the pinion is driven faster than the armature shaft. This causes the pinion to be screwed back along the sleeve and out of engagement with the flywheel. The main spring acts as a buffer when the pinion first takes up the driving torque and also acts as a buffer when the engine throws the pinion back out of mesh.

One of the main problems with this type of starter was the aggressive nature of the engagement. This tended to cause the pinion and ring gear to wear prematurely. In some applications the pinion tended to fall out of mesh when cranking due to the engine almost, but not quite, running. The pinion was also prone to seizure often due to contamination by dust from the clutch. This was often compounded by application of oil to the pinion mechanism, which tended to attract even more dust and thus prevent engagement. The pre-engaged starter motor has largely overcome these problems.

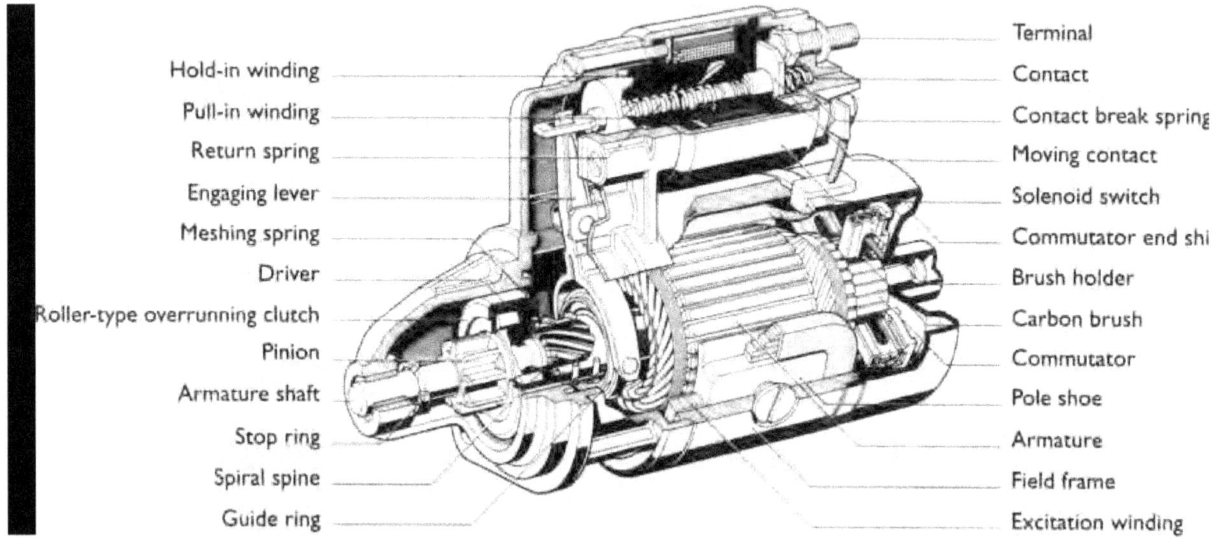

Pre-engaged starters

Pre-engaged starters are fitted to the majority of vehicles in use today. They provide a positive engagement with the ring gear, as full power is not applied until the pinion is fully in mesh. They prevent premature ejection as the pinion is held into mesh by the action of a solenoid. A one-way clutch is incorporated into the pinion to prevent the starter motor being driven by the engine. One example of a pre-engaged starter in common use is shown in Figure.

The basic operation of the pre-engaged starter is as follows. When the key switch is operated, a supply is made to terminal 50 on the solenoid. This causes two windings to be energized, the hold-on winding and the pull-in winding. Note that the pull-in winding is of very low resistance and hence a high current flows. This winding is connected in series with the motor circuit and the current flowing will allow the motor to rotate slowly to facilitate engagement. At the same time, the magnetism created in the solenoid attracts the plunger and, via an operating lever, pushes the pinion into mesh with the flywheel ring gear. When the pinion is fully in mesh the plunger, at the end of its travel, causes a heavy-duty set of copper contacts to close. These contacts now supply full battery power to the main circuit of the starter motor. When the main contacts are closed, the pull-in winding is effectively switched off due to equal voltage supply on both ends. The hold-on winding holds the plunger in position as long as the solenoid is supplied from the key switch. When the engine starts and the key is released, the main supply is removed and the plunger and pinion return to their rest positions under spring tension. A lost motion spring located on the plunger ensures that the main contacts open before the pinion is retracted from mesh.

During engagement, if the teeth of the pinion hit the teeth of the flywheel (tooth to tooth abutment), the main contacts are allowed to close due to the engagement spring being compressed. This allows the motor to rotate under power and the pinion will slip into mesh.

Figure shows a sectioned view of a one-way clutch assembly. The torque developed by the starter is passed through the clutch to the ring gear. The purpose of this free-wheeling device is to prevent the starter being driven at an excessively high speed if the pinion is held in mesh after the engine has started. The clutch consists of a driving and driven member with several rollers between the two. The rollers are spring loaded and either wedge-lock the two members together by being compressed against the springs, or free-wheel in the opposite direction. Many variations of the pre-engaged starter are in common use, but all work on similar lines to the above description. The wound field type of motor has now largely been replaced by the permanent magnet version.

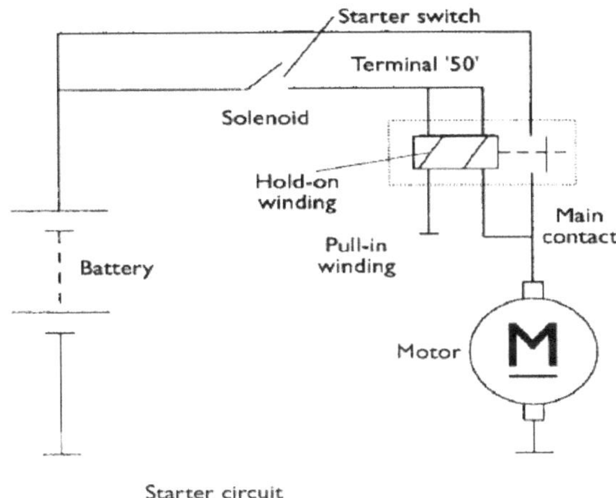

Starter circuit

Permanent magnet
starters

Permanent magnet starters began to appear on production vehicles in the late 1980s. The two main advantages of these motors, compared with conventional types, are less weight and smaller size. This makes the permanent magnet starter a popular choice by vehicle manufacturers as, due to the lower lines of today's cars, less space is now available for engine electrical systems. The reduction in weight provides a contribution towards reducing fuel consumption.

The standard permanent magnet starters currently available are suitable for use on spark ignition engines up to about 2 litre capacity. They are rated in the region of 1kW. The principle of operation is similar in most respects to the conventional pre-engaged starter motor. The main difference being the replacement of field windings and pole shoes with high quality permanent magnets. The reduction in weight is in the region of 15% and the diameter of the yoke can be reduced by a similar factor.

Permanent magnets provide constant excitation and it would be reasonable to expect the speed and torque characteristic to be constant. However, due to the fall in battery voltage under load and the low resistance of the armature windings, the characteristic is comparable to series wound motors. In some cases, flux concentrating pieces or interpoles are used between the main magnets. Due to the warping effect of the magnetic field, this tends to make the characteristic curve very similar to that of the series motor.

Development by some manufacturers has also taken place in the construction of the brushes. A copper and graphite mix is used but the brushes are made in two parts allowing a higher copper content in the power zone and a higher graphite content in the commutation zone. This results in increased service life and a reduction in voltage drop, giving improved starter power.

For applications with a higher power requirement, permanent magnet motors with intermediate transmission have been developed. These allow the armature to rotate at a higher and more efficient speed whilst still providing the torque, due to the gear reduction. Permanent magnet starters with intermediate transmission are available with power outputs of about 1.7 kW and are suitable for spark ignition engines up to about 3 litres, or compression ignition engines up to about 1.6 litres. This form of permanent magnet motor can give a weight saving of up to 40%. The principle of operation is again similar to the conventional pre-engaged starter. The intermediate transmission, is of the epicyclic type. The sun gear is on the armature shaft and the planet carrier drives the pinion. The ring gear or annulus remains stationary and also acts as an intermediate bearing. This arrangement of gears gives a reduction ratio of about 5 : 1. This can be calculated by the formula:

Ratio=AS/S

where A =number of teeth on the annulus, and

S =number of teeth on the sun gear.

The annulus gear in some types is constructed from a high grade polyamide compound with mineral additives to improve strength and wear resistance.

The sun and planet gears are conventional steel. This combination of materials gives a quieter and more efficient operation.

Heavy vehicle starters

The subject area of this book is primarily the electrical equipment on cars. This short section is included for interest, hence further reference should be made to other sources for greater detail about heavy vehicle starters.

The types of starter that are available for heavy duty applications are as many and varied as the applications they serve. In general, higher voltages are used, which may be up to 110 V in specialist cases, and two starters may even be running in parallel for very high power and torque requirements.

Large road vehicles are normally 24 V and employ a wide range of starters. In some cases the design is simply a large and heavy duty version of the pre-engaged type discussed earlier. This starter may also be fitted with a thermal cut-out to prevent overheating damage due to excessive cranking. Rated at 8.5kW, it is capable of producing over 80 Nm torque at 1000 rev/min. Other methods of engaging the pinion include sliding the whole armature or pushing the pinion with a rod through a hollow armature. This type uses a solenoid to push the pinion into mesh via a rod through the centre of the armature. Sliding-armature-type starters work by positioning the field windings forwards from the main armature body, such that the armature is attracted forwards when power is applied. A trip lever mechanism will then only allow full power when the armature has caused the pinion to mesh.

Integrated starters

A device called a 'dynastart' was used on a number of vehicles from the 1930s through to the 1960s.This device was a combination of the starter and a dynamo. The device, directly mounted on the crankshaft, was a compromise and hence not very efficient. The method is now known as an Integrated Starter Alternator Damper (ISAD). It consists of an electric motor, which functions as a control element between the engine and the transmission, and can also be used to start the engine and deliver electrical power to the batteries and the rest of the vehicle systems. The electric motor replaces the mass of the flywheel. The motor transfers the drive from the engine and is also able to act as a damper/vibration absorber unit. The damping effect is achieved by a rotation capacitor. A change in relative speed between the rotor and the engine due to the vibration, causes one pole of the capacitor to be charged. The effect of this is to take the energy from the vibration. Using ISAD to start the engine is virtually noiseless, and cranking speeds of 700 rev/min are possible. Even at _25 ° C it is still possible to crank at about 400 rev/min. A good feature of this is that a stop/start function is possible as an economy and emissions improvement technique. Because of the high speed cranking, the engine will fire up in about 0.1–0.5 seconds. The motor can also be used to aid with acceleration of the vehicle. This feature could be used to allow a smaller engine to be used or to enhance the performance of a standard engine.

When used in alternator mode, the ISAD can produce up to 2 kW at idle speed. It can supply power at different voltages as both AC and DC. Through the application of intelligent control electronics, the ISAD can be up to 80% efficient. Citroën have used the ISAD system in a Xsara model prototype. The car can produce 150 Nm for up to 30 seconds, which is significantly more than the 135 Nm peak torque of the 1580 cc, 65 kW fuel injected version. Citroën call the system 'Dynalto'. A 220 V outlet is even provided inside the car to power domestic electrical appliances!

Starter switches

An Ignition (or starter) switch is a switch in the control system of an internal combustion engined motor vehicle that activates the main electrical systems for the vehicle. Besides providing power to the starter solenoid and the ignition system components (including the engine control unit and ignition coil) it also usually switches on power to many "accessories" (radio, power windows, etc.). The ignition switch usually requires a key be inserted that works a lock built into the switch mechanism. It is frequently combined with the starter switch which activates the starter motor. The ignition locking system may be bypassed by disconnecting the wiring to the switch and manipulating it directly; this is known as hotwiring.

Regulation of output voltage

To prevent the vehicle battery from being overcharged the regulated system voltage should be kept below the gassing voltage of the lead-acid battery. A figure of 14.2 +/- 0.2 V is used for all 12 V charging systems. Accurate voltage control is vital with the ever-increasing use of electronic systems. It has also enabled the wider use of sealed batteries, as the possibility of over-charging is minimal. Figure 6.15 shows two common voltage regulators. Voltage regulation is a difficult task on a vehicle alternator because of the constantly changing engine speed and loads on the alternator. The output of an alternator without regulation would rise linearly in proportion with engine speed. Alternator output is also proportional to magnetic field strength and this, in turn, is proportional to the field current. It is the task of the regulator to control this field current in response to alternator output voltage. Figure 6.16 shows a flow chart which

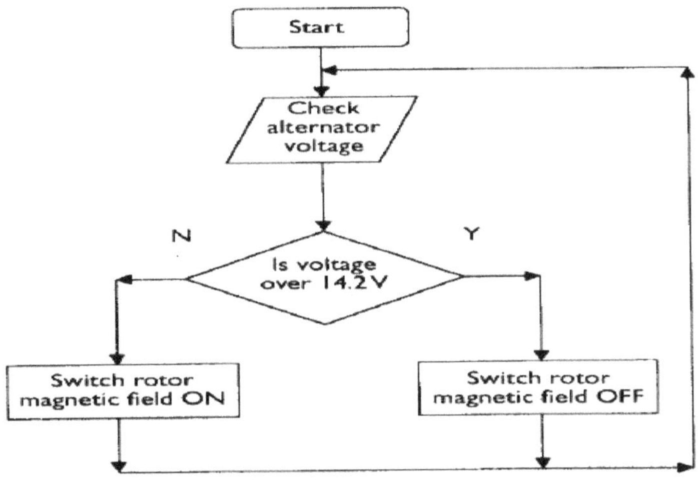

Figure 6.16 Action of the voltage regulator

Figure 6.19 Electronic voltage regulator

represents the action of the regulator, showing how the field current is switched off as output voltage increases and then back on again as output voltage falls. The abrupt switching of the field current does not cause abrupt changes in output voltage due to the very high inductance of the field (rotor) windings. In addition, the whole

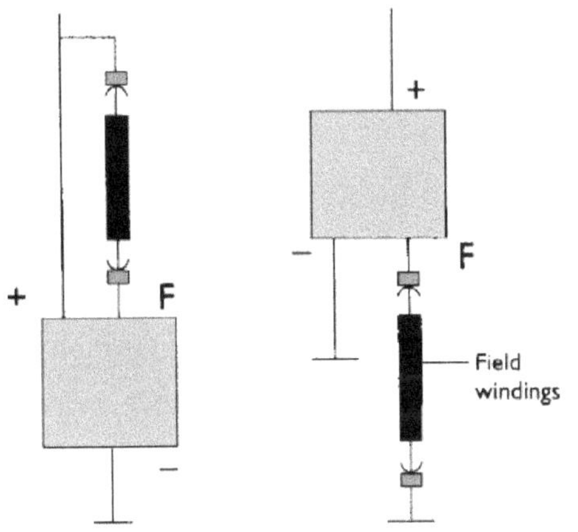

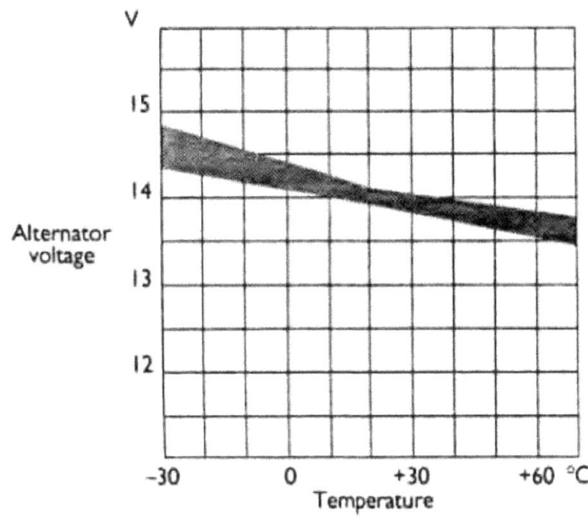

Figure 6.17 How the voltage regulator is incorporated in the field circuit

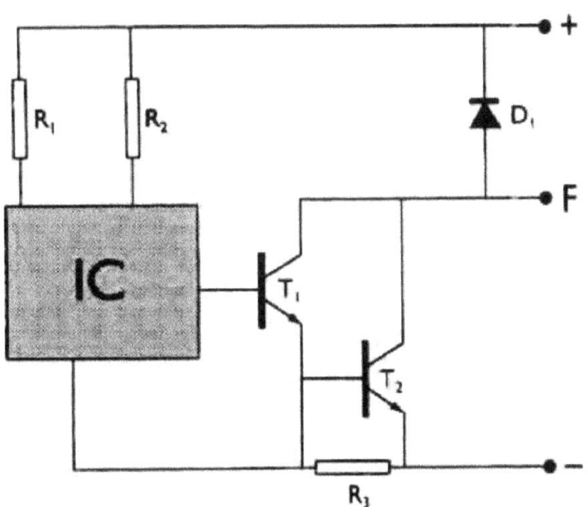

Figure 6.21 How the regulator response changes with temperature

switching process only takes a few milliseconds. Many regulators also incorporate some temperature compensation to allow

a higher charge rate in colder conditions and to reduce the rate in hot conditions.

Figure 6.20 Hybrid IC regulator circuit

When working with regulator circuits, care must be taken to note 'where' the field circuit is interrupted. For example, some alternator circuits supply a constant feed to the field windings from the excitation diodes and the regulator switches the earth side. In other systems, one side of the field windings is will switch off, allowing T2 to switch back on and so the cycle will continue. The conventional diode, D1, absorbs the back EMF from the field windings and so prevents damage to the other components. Electronic regulators can be made to sense either the battery voltage, the machine voltage (alternator), or a combination of the two. Most systems in use at present tend to be machine sensed as this offers some protection against over-voltage in the event of the alternator being driven with the battery disconnected. Figure 6.20 shows the circuit of a hybrid integrated circuit (IC) voltage regulator. The hybrid system involves the connection of discrete components on a ceramic plate using film techniques. The main part of the regulator is an integrated circuit containing the sensing elements and temperature compensation components. The IC controls an output stage such as a Darlington pair. This technique produces a very compact device and, because of the low number of components and connections, is very reliable. Figure 6.21 is a graph showing how the IC regulator response changes with temperature. This change is important to ensure correct charging under 'summer' and 'winter' conditions. When a battery is cold, the electrolyte resistance increases. This means a higher voltage is necessary to cause the correct recharging current. Over-voltage protection is required in some applications in order to prevent damage to electronic components. When an alternator is connected to a vehicle battery system, the voltage, even in the event of regulator failure, will not often exceed about 20V due to the low resistance and swamping effect of the battery. If an alternator is run with the battery disconnected (which is not recommended), a heavy duty Zener diode connected across the output of the WL/field diodes will offer some protection as, if the system voltage exceeds its breakdown figure, it will conduct and cause the system voltage to be kept within reasonable limits.

Charging circuits

For many applications, the charging circuit is one of the simplest on the vehicle. The main output is connected to the battery via a suitably sized cable (or in some cases two cables to increase reliability and flexibility), and the warning light is connected to an ignition supply on one side and to the alternator terminal at the other. A wire may also be connected to the phase terminal if it is utilized. Figure 6.22 shows two typical wiring circuits. Note that the output of the alternator is often connected to the starter main supply simply for convenience of wiring. If the wires are kept as short as possible this will reduce voltage drop in the circuit. The voltage drop across the main supply wire when the alternator is producing full output current, should be less than 0.5V.

Some systems have an extra wire from the alternator to 'sense' battery voltage directly. An ignition feed may also be found and this is often used to ensure instant excitement of the field windings. A number of vehicles link a wire from the engine management ECU to the alternator. This is used to send a signal to increase engine idle speed if the battery is low on charge.

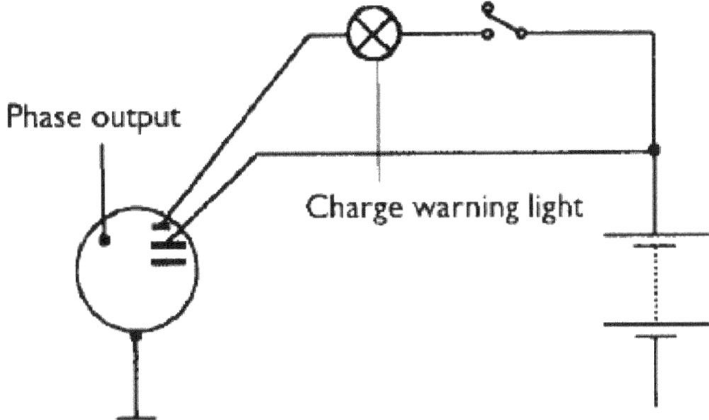

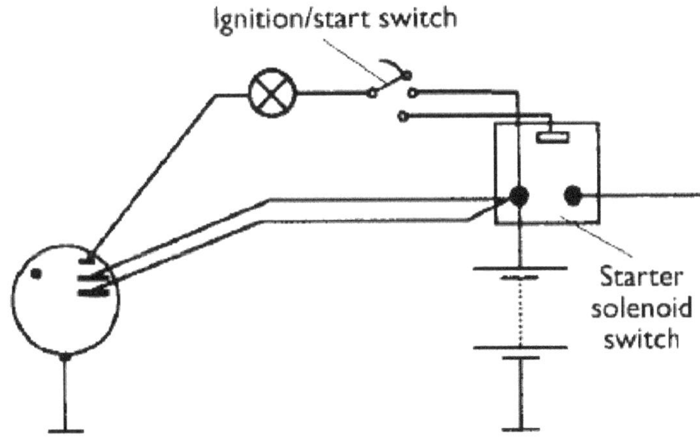

Figure 6.22 Example charging circuits

CUTOUT RELAY

The cutout relay (Figs. 2 & 3) has two windings, a series winding of a few turns of heavy wire (shown in solid red) and a shunt winding of many turns of fine wire (shown in dashed red). The shunt winding is connected across the generator so that generator voltage is impressed upon it at all times.

The series winding is connected in series with the charging circuit so that all generator output passes through it. The relay core and windings are assembled into a frame. A flat steel armature is attached to the frame by a flexible hinge so that it is centered just above the end of the core. The armature contact points are located just above the stationary contact points. When the generator is not operating, the armature contact points are held a wax from the stationary points by the tension of a flat spring riveted on the side of the armature.

CUTOUT RELAY ACTION-When the generator voltage builds up a value great enough to charge the battery, the magnetism induced by the relay windings is sufficient to pull the armature toward the core so that the contact points close. This com- pletes the circuit between the generator and battery. The current which flows from the generator to the battery passes through the series winding in a direction to add to the magnetism holding the armature down and the contact points closed.

When the' generator slows down or stops, current begins to flow from the battery to the generator. This reverse flow of current through the series winding causes a reversal of the series winding magnetic field. The magnetic field of the shunt winding does not reverse. Therefore, instead of helping each other, the two windings now magnetically oppose so that the resultant magnetic field becomes insufficient to hold the armature down. The flat spring pulls the armature away from the core so that the points separate; this opens the circuit between the generator and battery.

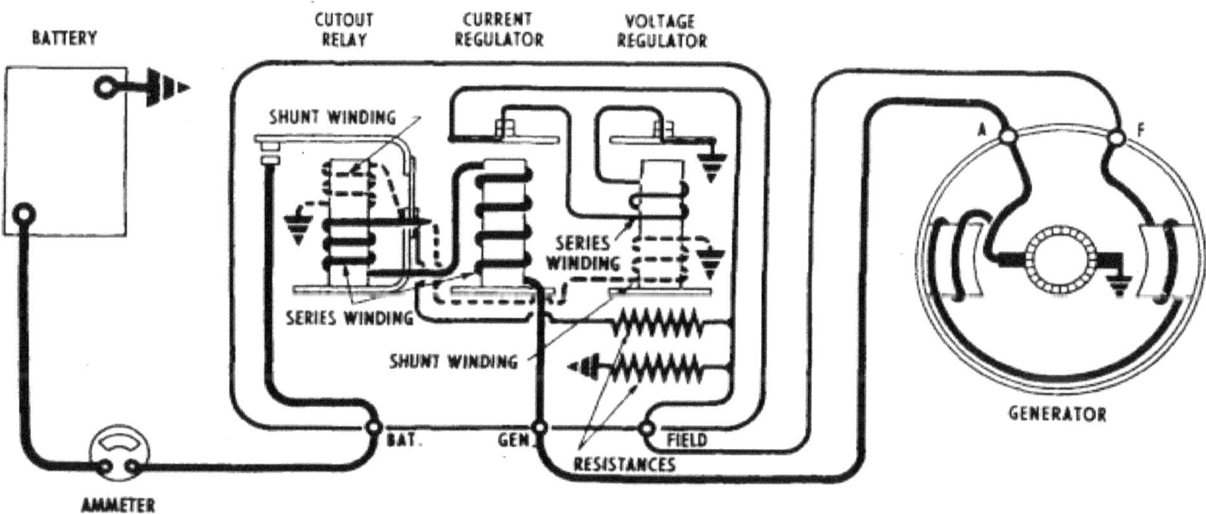

Figure 2—Wiring circuit of Delco-Remy grounded type, three-unit regulator shown in Figure 1. The shunt windings in the cutout relay and voltage regulator are shown in dashed red. The series windings in the cutout relay and current regulator are shown in solid red. The series winding in the voltage regulator is shown in blue.

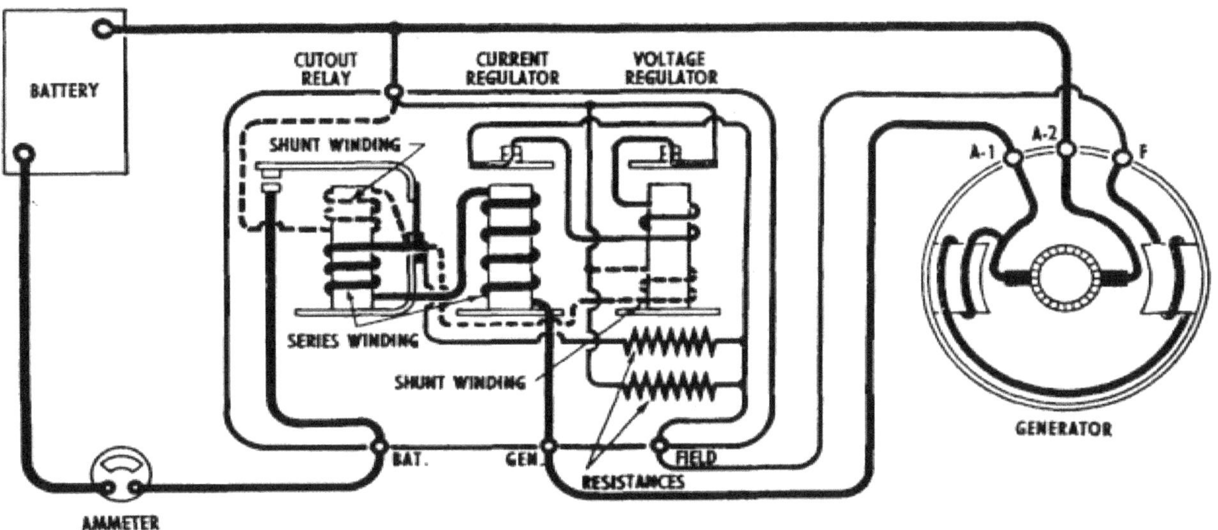

Figure 3—Wiring Circuit of Delco-Remy insulated type, three-unit regulator similar to that shown in Figure 1. The shunt windings in the cutout relay and voltage regulator are shown in dashed red. The series windings in the cutout relay and current regulator are shown in solid red. The series winding in the voltage regulator is shown in blue.

VOLTAGE REGULATOR

The voltage regulator (Figs. 2 & 3) has two windings assembled on a single core, a shunt winding consisting of many turns of fine wire (shown in dashed red) which is shunted across the generator, and a series winding of a few turns of relatively heavy wire (shown in solid blue) which is connected in series with the generator field circuit when the regulator contact points are closed.

The windings and core are assembled into a frame. A flat steel armature is attached to the frame by a flexible hinge so that it is just above the end of the core. The armature contains a contact point which is just beneath a stationary contact point. When the voltage regulator is not operating, the tension of a spiral spring holds the armature away from the core so that the points are in contact and the generator field circuit is completed to ground through them.

VOLTAGE REGULATOR ACTION-When the generator voltage reaches the value for which the voltage regulator is adjusted, the magnetic field produced by the two windings (shunt and series) overcomes the armature spring tension and pulls the armature down so that the contact points separate. This inserts resistance into the generator field circuit so that the generator field current and voltage are reduced. Reduction of the generator voltage reduces the magnetic field of the regulator shunt winding. Also, opening the regulator points opens the regulator series winding circuit so that its magnetic field collapses completely. The consequence is that the magnetic field is reduced sufficiently to allow the spiral spring to pull the armature away from the core so that the contact points again close. This directly grounds the generator field circuit so that generator voltage and output increase. The above cycle of action again takes place and the cycle continues at a rate of 50 to 200 times a second, regulating the voltage to a predetermined value. With the voltage thus limited the generator supplies varying amounts of current to meet the varying states of battery charge and electrical load.

Solenoid

A solenoid is simply a specially designed electromagnet. A solenoid usually consists of a cylindrical coil wound with one or more layers of insulated wire and a movable iron core called the *armature*. When current flows through a wire, a magnetic field is set up around the wire. If we make a coil of many turns of wire, this magnetic field becomes many times stronger, flowing around the coil and through its center in a doughnut shape. The length of the solenoid is much larger in comparison with its diameter. When the coil of the solenoid is energized with current, the core moves to increase the flux linkage by closing the air gap between the cores. The movable core is usually spring-loaded to allow the core to retract when the current is switched off. The force generated is approximately proportional to the square of the current and inversely proportional to the square of the length of the air gap.

Solenoids are inexpensive, and their use is primarily limited to on-off applications such as latching, locking, and triggering. They are frequently used in home appliances (e.g. washing machine valves), office equipment (e.g. copy machines), automobiles (e.g. door latches and the starter solenoid), pinball machines (e.g., plungers and bumpers), and factory automation.

Flux Distribution of a Solenoid

The direction of the field inside the solenoid may be found by applying the right hand rule for solenoids. This rule states that if a solenoid is grasped with the right hand such that the fingers point in the direction of the current in the wire, then the thumb will point in the direction of magnetic flux. The application of the right hand rule for solenoids is illustrated in figure 1.1. The flux distribution due to solenoid carrying current is given in figure 1.2. The magnetic field produced by a solenoid is similar to that of a bar magnet. One end of the solenoid becomes a north pole (N) where the flux leaves the solenoid. The other end becomes the South Pole (S) where the flux enters it.

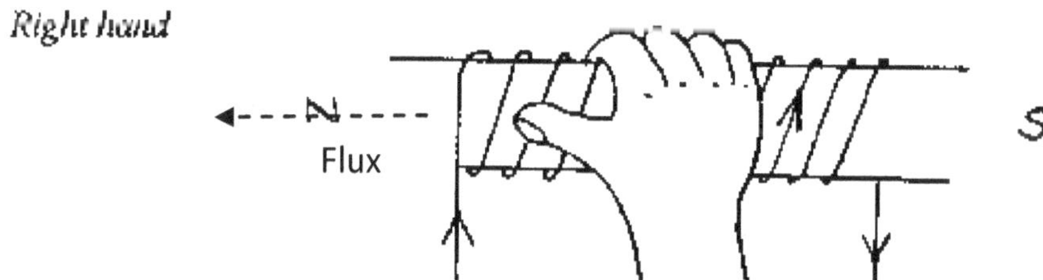

Figure 1.1 Right hand rule for solenoid

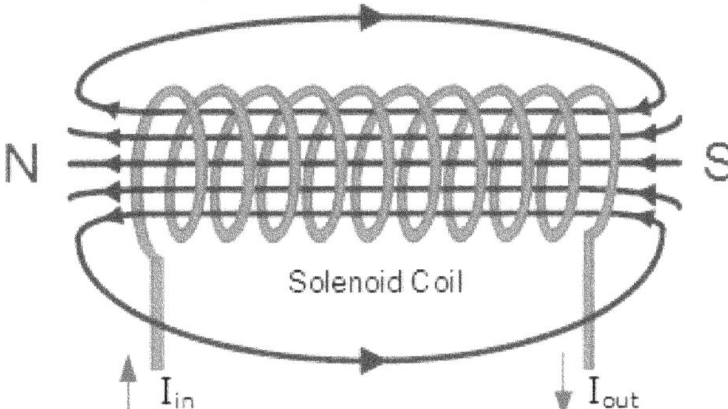

Figure 1.2 Magnetic field due to a solenoid carrying current

<u>Application of Solenoid</u>

An electromechanical *relay* is a solenoid used to make or break mechanical contact between electrical leads. A small voltage input to the solenoid controls a potentially large current through the relay contacts. Applications include power switches and electromechanical control elements. A relay performs a function similar to a power transistor but has the capability to switch extremely large currents if necessary. However, transistors have a much shorter switching time than relays.

As illustrated in figure 2, a *voice coil* consists of a coil that moves in a magnetic field produced by a permanent magnet and intensified by an iron core. The force on the coil is directly proportional to the current in the coil. The coil is usually attached to a movable load such as the diaphragm of an audio speaker, the spool of a hydraulic proportional valve, or the read-write head of a computer disk drive. The linear response and bidirectional capability make voice coils more attractive than solenoids for control applications.

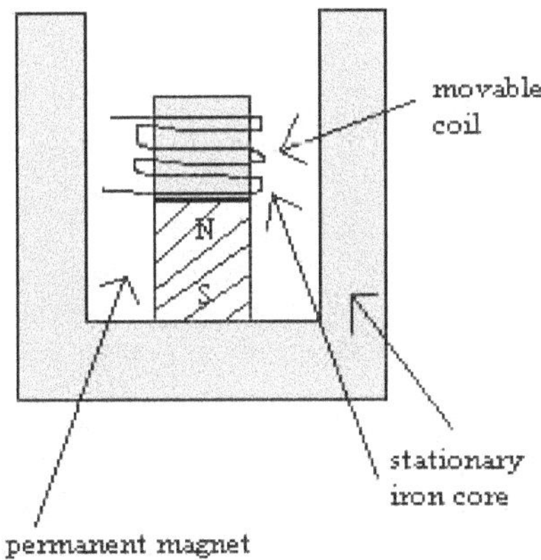

Fig 2. Voice coil

Charging System Components

The Charging system is an important part of the electrical system. The charging system has two essential functions:

- Generate electrical power to run the vehicle's electrical systems
- Generate current to recharge the vehicle's battery

Electrical Power: At low engine speeds, the battery may supply some of the power the vehicle needs. At high engine speeds, the charging system handles all of the vehicle's electrical requirements.

Charging: Alternator (generator) output is higher than battery voltage to recharge the battery.

The charging system components:

These components make up the charging system:

- Alternator
- Voltage regulator
- Battery
- Charging Indicator

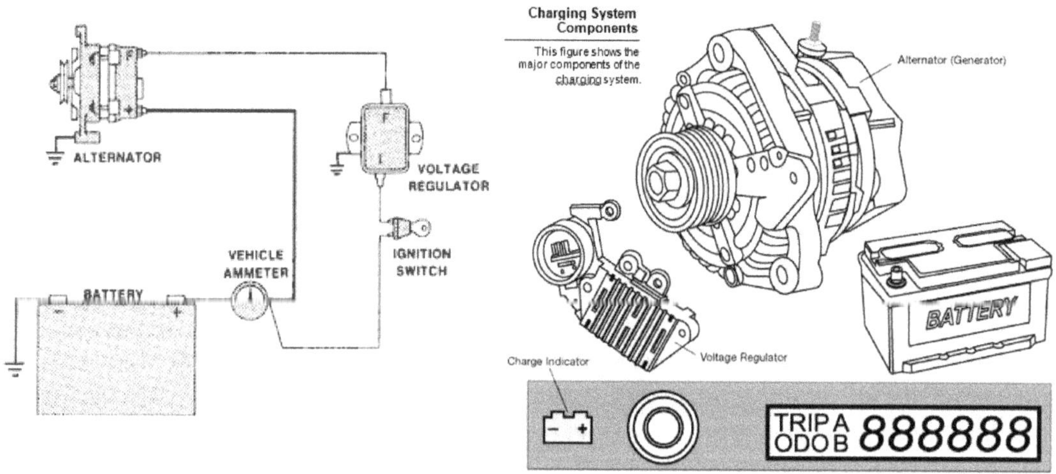

I.   Alternator

The alternator generates electrical power to run accessories and to recharge the batteries. It is normally driven by a belt located off the crankshaft. Mechanical energy from the crankshaft is converted by the alternator into electrical energy for the batteries and accessories.
The alternator contains three main components:
- Stator (attached to alternator housing, remains stationary),

- Rotor (spins inside the stator),
- Rectifier,

Slip ring and brushes make an electrical connection to the spinning rotor.

The alternator generates electricity through these steps:
- Engine power drives the alternator rotor through a pulley and drive belt.
- The alternator rotor spins inside the windings of the stator.
- The stator windings generate an alternating current.
- Rectifier diodes change the alternating current (AC) into direct current (DC).

II.   Voltage regulator

The voltage regulator acts as an electrical traffic cop to control alternator output. It senses when the batteries need recharging, or when the vehicles electrical needs increase, and adjusts the alternators output accordingly. ie., it controls the alternator's output current to prevent over-charging and under charging of the battery. It does this by regulating the current flowing from the battery to the rotor's field coil.

The voltage regulator can be mounted inside or outside of the alternator housing. If the regulator is mounted outside there will be a wiring harness connecting it to the alternator. Today's IC voltage regulator is a fully electronic device, using resistors and diodes.

III.   Battery

The batteries are a reservoir of chemical electrical power. Their primary purpose is to crank the engine. They also supply power to vehicle accessories when the electrical load is too great for the alternator alone. The battery also acts as a voltage stabilizer. The battery must always remain attached to the electrical system while the engine is running.

IV.   Charging Indicator

The charging indicator is usually an ON /OFF warning lamp. When the system is running, the light should be off. The lamp lights when the charging system is not providing sufficient charge.

Synchronous generator (Alternators)

AC generators are usually called alternators. They are also called synchronous generators. A synchronous generator is a machine for converting mechanical power from a prime mover to ac electric power at a specific voltage and frequency.

Principle of Operation: The operation of a synchronous generator is based on Faraday's law of electromagnetic induction, and in an ac synchronous generator the generation of emf's is by relative motion of conductors and magnetic flux. The rotating magnetic field induces an AC voltage in the stator windings. Since the currents in the stator windings vary in step with the position of the rotor, an alternator is a synchronous generator.

In constructing a synchronous machine a point to note is that the stator is fixed and the poles rotate.

There are two categories of Synchronous machines:
(a) those with salient or projecting poles
(b) those with cylindrical rotors

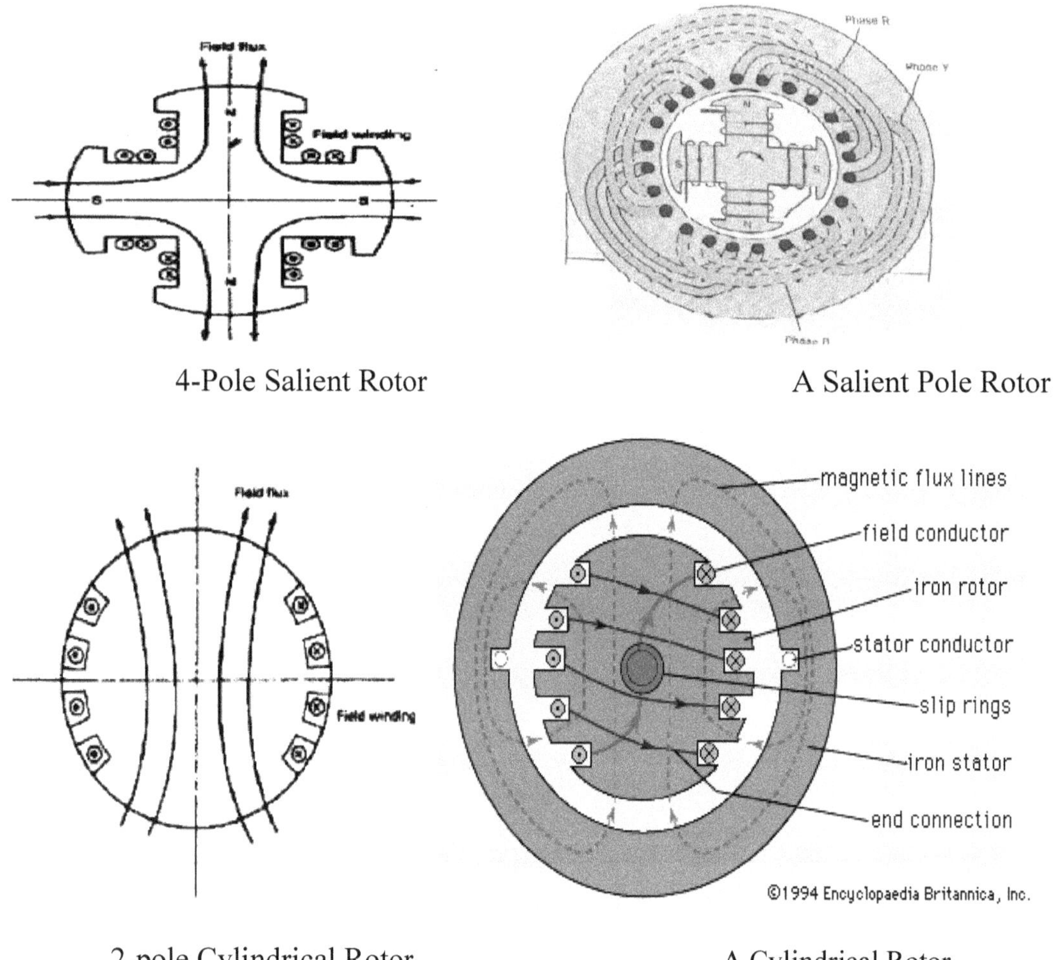

<table>
<tr><td align="center">4-Pole Salient Rotor</td><td align="center">A Salient Pole Rotor</td></tr>
<tr><td align="center">2-pole Cylindrical Rotor</td><td align="center">A Cylindrical Rotor</td></tr>
</table>

<u>**Single Phase Alternator**</u>

- Single-phase alternator is an <u>alternating current</u> <u>electrical generator</u> that produces a single, continuously alternating voltage. Single-phase generators can be used to generate power in <u>single-phase electric power</u> systems.
- A single-phase alternator has all the armature conductors connected in series
- The stator is two poles. The winding is wound in two distinct pole groups, both poles being wound in the same direction around the stator frame.
- The rotor also consists of two pole groups, adjacent poles being of opposite polarity.

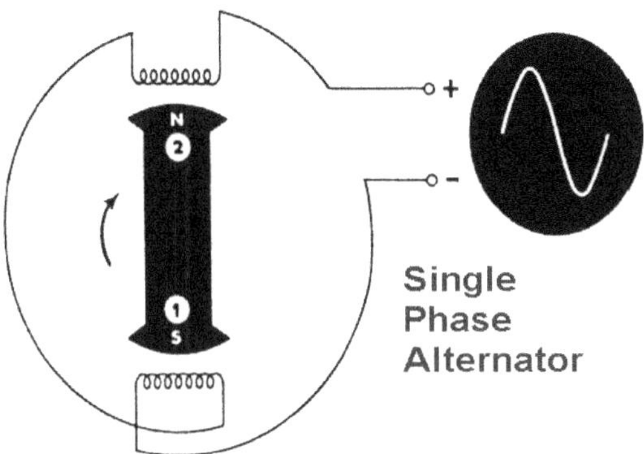

- The two poles of the stator winding are connected to each other so that the AC voltages are in phase, so they add.
- As the rotor (field) turns, its poles will induce AC voltages in the stator (armature) windings. Since one rotor pole is in the same position relative to a stator pole as any other rotor pole, both the stator poles are cut by equal amounts of magnetic lines of force at any time. As a result, the voltages induced in the two poles of the stator winding have the same amplitude or value at any given instant.

Three Phase Alternator

- The three-phase alternator has three single-phase windings spaced so that the voltage induced in any one is phase-displaced by 120 degrees from the other two.
- The voltage waveforms generated across each phase are drawn on a graph phase-displaced 120 degrees from each other.

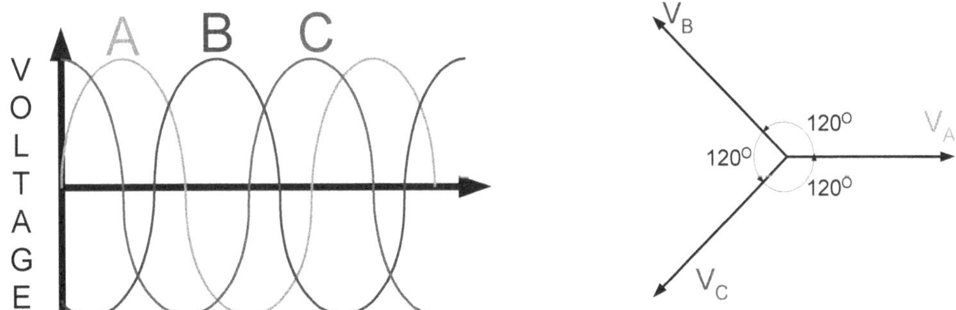

- The three phases are independent of each other.
- One point from each winding can be connected to form a neutral and thus make a wye (star) connection.
- The voltage from this point to any one of the line leads will be the phase voltage. The line voltage across any two line leads is the vector sum of the individual phase voltages. The line voltage is 1.73, ($\sqrt{3}$), times the phase voltage.
- Since the windings form only one path for current flow between phases, the line and phase currents are equal.

- A three-phase stator can also be connected so that the phases form a "delta" connection.

- In the delta connection the line voltages are equal to the phase voltages, but the line currents will be equal to the vector sum of the phase currents.

- Since the phases are 120 degrees out of phase, the line current will be 1.73, ($\sqrt{3}$), times the phase current. Both "star" and the "delta" connections are used in alternators.

<u>Three Phase Stator Connection</u>

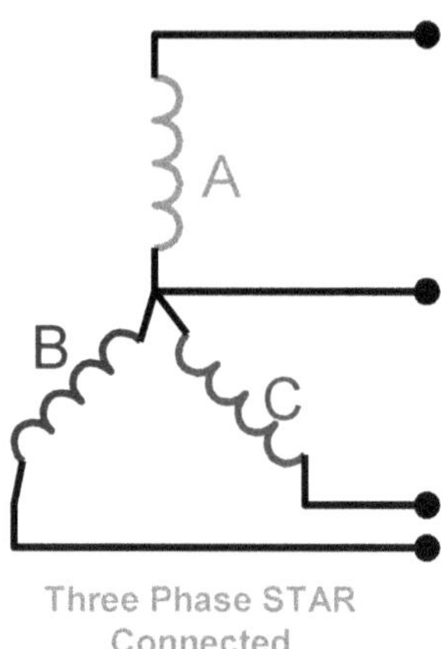

- The frequency of the AC generated by an alternator depends upon the number of poles and the speed of the rotor

- When a rotor has rotated through an angle so that two adjacent rotor poles (a north and a south) have passed one winding, the voltage induced in that one winding will have varied through a complete cycle of 360 electrical degrees.

- A two pole machine must rotate at twice the speed of a four-pole machine to generate the same frequency.

- The magnitude of the voltage generated by an alternator can be varied by adjusting the current on the rotor which changes the strength of the magnetic field.

- A two pole alternator produces one electrical cycle for each complete mechanical rotation.

- A four pole alternator will produce two electrical cycles for each mechanical rotation because two north and two south poles move by each winding on the stator for one complete revolution of the rotor.

- $f = (N)(P/2)/60 = (NP)/120$

  where N is the speed of the rotor in revolutions per minute,

P is the number of poles

f is the electrical line frequency produced by the alternator.

- The speed of the rotor must be divided by 60 to change from revolutions per minute to revolutions per second.

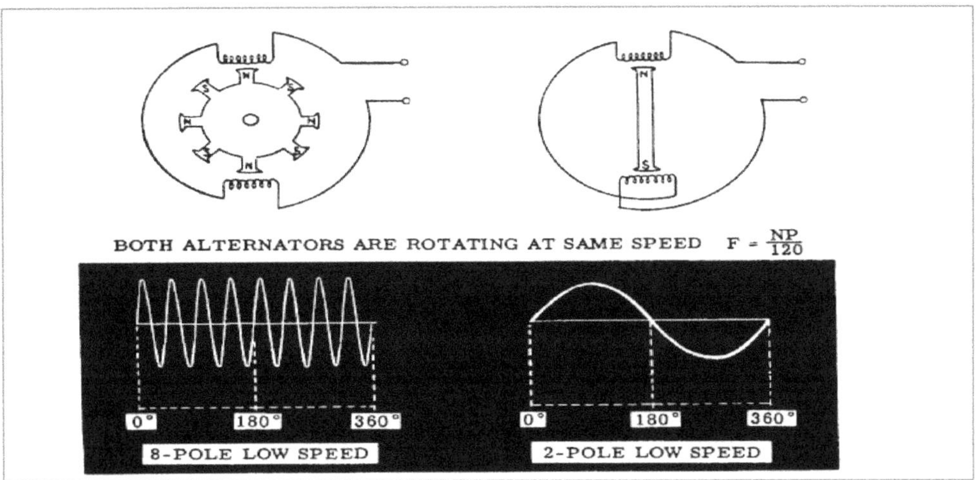

- In an alternator the output voltage varies with the load.

- There are two voltage drops.{ IR & IX_L }

- The IX_L drop is due to the inductive reactance of the armature windings.

- Both the IR drop and the IXL drop decrease the output voltage as the load increases.

- The change in voltage from no-load to full-load is called the "voltage regulation" of an alternator.

- A constant voltage output from an alternator is maintained by varying the field strength as required by changes in load.

EMF Equation of an alternator

Let,
P= No. of poles
Z= No. of Conductors or Coil sides in series/phase i.e. Z= 2T
where T is the number of coils or turns per phase
f = frequency of induced e.m.f in Hz
ϕ = Flux per pole (Weber)
N = rotor speed (RPM)

If induced e.m.f is assumed sinusoidal then, K_f= Form factor = 1.11

In one revolution of the rotor i.e. in 60/N seconds, each conductor is cut by a flux of Pϕ Webers.

dϕ= ϕP and also dt= seconds60/N

then induced e.m.f per conductor (average) = dϕ/ dt= Pϕ/(60/N) =P N ϕ/60   .....(a)

But We know that f = PN/120 or N= 120f/P

Putting the value of N in Equation (a)...

We get the average value of e.m.f per conductor is

Eav = Pϕ/60 x 120 f/P = **2f ϕ Volts.**   {N= 120f/P}

If there are Z conductors in series per phase,

 then average e.m.f per phase = 2fϕZ Volts= ***4fϕT Volts*** ....{Z=2T}

Also we know that Form factor= RMS Value/Average Value...

= RMS value= Form factor x Average Value,

= 1.11 x 4fϕT = <u>4.44fϕT Volts.</u>

<u>GENERATORS</u>

<u>Construction of DC Generator</u>

In construction dc machine consists of four parts mainly, 1. Field magnets 2. Armature 3. Commutator 4. Brush and brush gear. DC machine (can be a generator or motor) with four poles is shown in figure 1.1

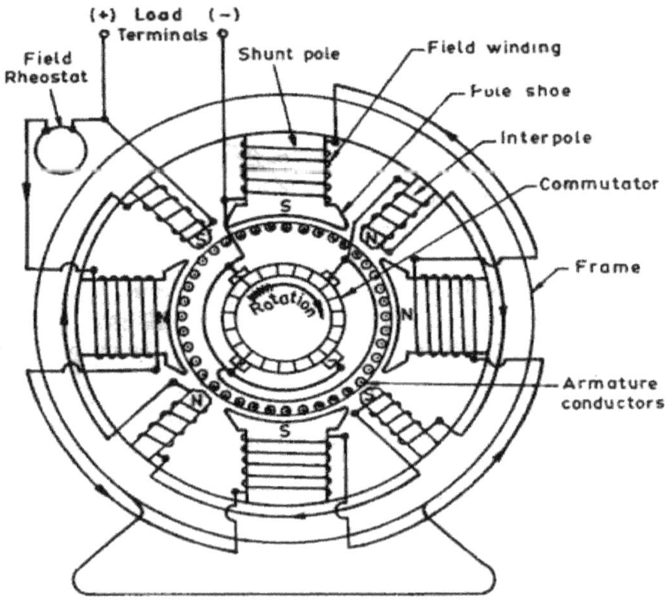

1. Field System:

The object of the field system is to create a uniform magnetic field within with the armature rotates. Electromagnets are preferred on the account of their magnetic effects and field strength regulation which can be achieved by controlling the magnetizing current. Field magnets consist of the following parts:

(i) Yoke or Frame   (ii) Pole cores   (iii) Pole shoes   (iv) Magnetizing coils

Cylindrical yoke is usually used which acts as a frame of the machine and carries the magnetic flux produced by the poles. Since the field is stationary there is no need to use laminated yoke for normal machine. In small machines, cast iron yokes are used because of its cheapness but yoke of large machines are made of fabricated steel due to its high permeability.

Pole core is usually of circular section and is used to carry the coils of insulated wires carrying the exciting current. Pole cores are usually not laminated and made of cast steel.

Each pole core has a pole shoe serves having a curved surface. The pole shoe serves two purposes:

(i)   It supports the field coils
(ii)   It increases the cross-sectional area of the magnetic circuit and reduces its reluctance.

Each pole core has one or more field coils or magnetizing coils placed over it to produce a magnetic field. The field coils are connected in series with one another such that when the current flows through the coils, alternate north and south poles are produced in the direction of rotation.

2. Armature

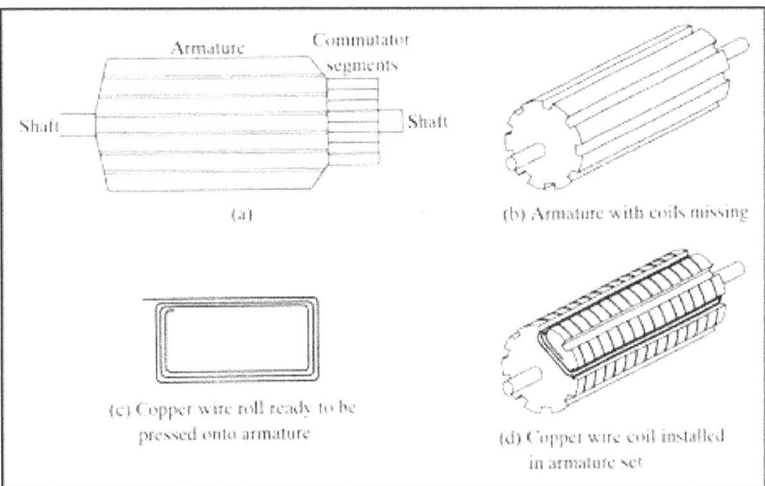

It is a rotating part of a DC machine and is built up in a cylindrical or drum shape. The purpose of armature is to rotate the conductors in the uniform magnetic field. It consists of coils of insulated wires wound around an iron and so arranged that electric currents are induced in these wires when the armature is rotated in a magnetic field. Its most important function is to provide a path of low reluctance to the magnetic flux. The armature core is made of high permeability silicon-steel stampings.

3. Commutator:

It is a form of rotating switch. They are placed between armature and external circuit. The commutator will reverse the connections to the external circuit at the instant aech reversal of circuit in the armature coil.

4. Brushes & Bearings

Brushes are made of carbon or graphite. It collects current from the commutator and convey it to external load resistance. It is rectangular in shape. Brushes are housed in brush holders and mounted over brush holder studs. Ball bearings are used as they are reliable for light machines.For heavy machines roller bearings are used.

<u>Working Principle:</u>

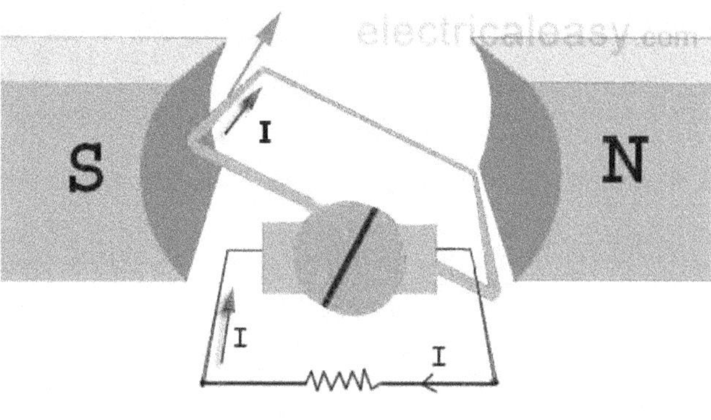

(a)

(b) According to Faraday's law of electromagnetic induction, when a conductor moves in a magnetic field (thereby cutting the magnetic flux lines), a dynamically induced emf is produced in the conductor. The magnitude of generated emf can be given by emf equation of DC generator. If a closed path is provided to the moving conductor then generated emf causes a current to flow in the circuit.

(c) Thus in DC generators, as we have studied earlier, when armature is rotated with the help of a prime mover and field windings are excited (there may be permanent field magnets also), emf is induced in armature conductors. This induced emf is taken out via commutator-brush arrangement.

E.M.F Equation of a DC Generator
Let

Φ = flux/pole in weber

Z = total number of armture conductors

= No.of slots x No.of conductors/slot

P = No.of generator poles

A = No.of parallel paths in armature

N = armature rotation in revolutions per minute (r.p.m)

E = e.m.f induced in any parallel path in armature

Generated e.m.f Eg = e.m.f generated in any one of the parallel paths i.e E.

Average e.m.f geneated /conductor = $\mathbf{d\Phi/dt}$ volt (n=1)

Now, flux cut/conductor in one revolution $\mathbf{d\Phi = \Phi P}$ Wb

No.of revolutions/second = N/60

Time for one revolution, $\mathbf{dt = 60/N}$ second

Hence, according to Faraday's Laws of Electroagnetic Induction,

E.M.F generated/conductor is

$$\frac{d\varnothing}{dt} = \frac{\varnothing\, PN}{60}$$

For a simplex wave-wound generator

No.of parallel paths = 2

No.of conductors (in series) in one path = Z/2

E.M.F. generated/path is

$$\frac{\varnothing\, PN}{60} \times \frac{Z}{2} = \frac{\varnothing ZPN}{120} \text{ volt}$$

For a simplex lap-wound generator

No.of parallel paths = P

No.of conductors (in series) in one path = Z/P

E.M.F.generated/path

$$\frac{\varnothing\, PN}{60} \times \frac{Z}{P} = \frac{\varnothing ZN}{60} \text{ volt}$$

In general generated e.m.f

$$E_g = \frac{\varnothing ZN}{60} \times \left(\frac{P}{A}\right) \text{ volt}$$

where A = 2 for simplex wave-winding

and A= P for simplex lap-winding

Types of Generators

Generators are usually classified according to the way in which their fields are excited.The field windings provide the excitation necessary to set up the magnetic fields in the machine. There are various types of field windings that can be used in the generator or motor circuit. In addition to the following field winding types, permanent magnet fields are used on some smaller DC products.

Generators may be divided in to
(a) Separately-excited generators
(b) Self-excited generators.

Separately-excited generators are those whoe field magnets are energised from an independent external source of DC current.

Self-excited generators are those whose field magnets are energused by the current produced by the generators themselves.Due to residual magnetism, there is always present someflux in the poles.When the armature is rotated, some e.m.f and hence some induced current is produced which is partly or fully passed through the field coils thereby strengthening the residual pole flux.

Self-excited generators are classed according to the type of field connection they use. There are three general types of field connections —
SERIES-WOUND, SHUNT-WOUND (parallel), and COMPOUND-WOUND.
Compound-wound generators are further classified as cumulative-compound and differential-compound.

Series-wound generator

In the series-wound generator, shown in figure, the field windings are connected in series with the armature. Current that flows in the armature flows through the external circuit and through the field windings. The external circuit connected to the generator is called the load circuit

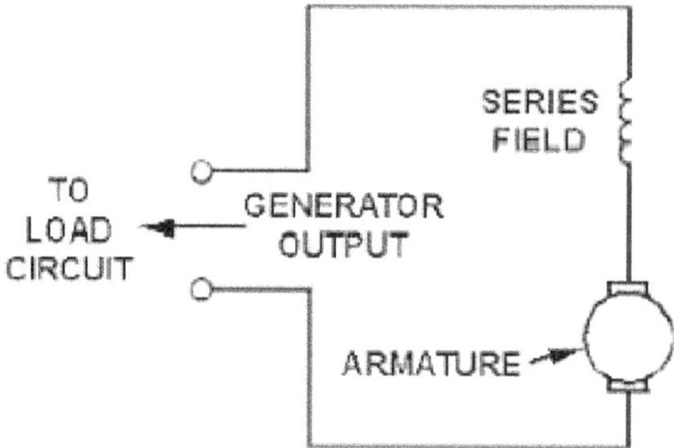

A series-wound generator uses very low resistance field coils, which consist of a few turns of large diameter wire.

The voltage output increases as the load circuit starts drawing more current. Under low-load current conditions, the current that flows in the load and through the generator is small. Since small current means that a small magnetic field is set up by the field poles, only a small voltage is induced in the armature. If the resistance of the load decreases, the load current increases.

Under this condition, more current flows through the field. This increases the magnetic field and increases the output voltage. A series-wound dc generator has the characteristic that the output voltage varies with load current. This is undesirable in most applications. For this reason, this type of generator is rarely used in everyday practice.

Shunt wound
In this field winding is connected in parallel with the armature conductors and have the full voltage of the generator applied across them.The field coils consist of many turns of small wire. They are connected in parallel with the load. In other words, they are connected across the output voltage of the armature.

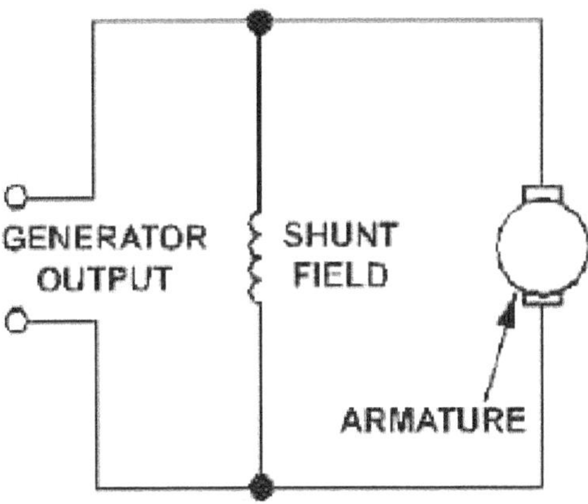

Current in the field windings of a shunt-wound generator is independent of the load current (currents in parallel branches are independent of each other). Since field current, and therefore field strength, is not affected by load current, the output voltage remains more nearly constant than does the output voltage of the series-wound generator.

In actual use, the output voltage in a dc shunt-wound generator varies inversely as load current varies. The output voltage decreases as load current increases because the voltage drop across the armature resistance increases ($E = IR$).

In a series-wound generator, output voltage varies directly with load current. In the shunt-wound generator, output voltage varies inversely with load current. A combination of the two types can overcome the disadvantages of both. This combination of windings is called the compound-wound dc generator.

Compound-wound generator :
Compound-wound generators have a series-field winding in addition to a shunt-field winding, as shown in figure.

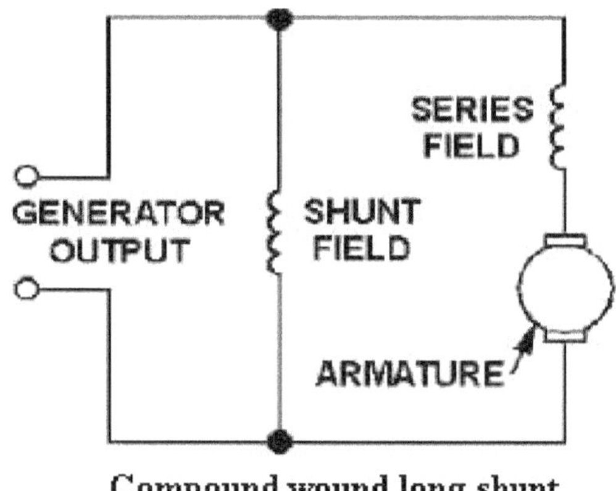

Compound wound long shunt

The shunt and series windings are wound on the same pole pieces. They can be either short-shunt or long-shunt as shown in figures. In a comound generator, the shunt field is stronger than the series field.When series field aids the shunt field, generator is said to be commutatively-compounded.On the other hand if series field opposes the shunt field,the generator is said to be differentially compounded.

In the compound-wound generator when load current increases, the armature voltage decreases just as in the shunt-wound generator. This causes the voltage applied to the shunt-field winding

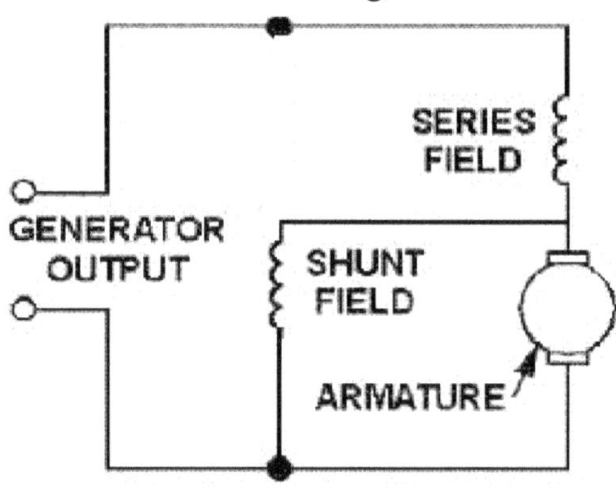

Compound wound short shunt

to   decrease, which results in a decrease in the magnetic field. This same increase in load current, since it flows through the series winding, causes an increase in the magnetic field produced by that winding.

By proportioning the two fields so that the decrease in the shunt field is just compensated by the increase in the series field, the output voltage remains constant. This is shown in figure, which shows the voltage characteristics of the series-, shunt-, and compound-wound generators. As you can see, by proportioning the effects of the two fields (series and shunt), a compound-wound generator provides a constant output voltage under varying load conditions. Actual curves are

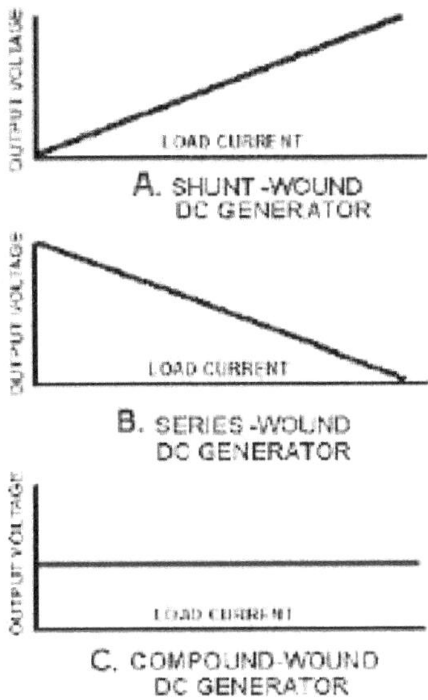

Voltage output characteristics

seldom, if ever, as perfect as shown.

<u>Characteristics of DC generators</u>

The speed of a d.c. machine operated as a generator is fixed by the prime mover. For general-purpose operation, the prime mover is equipped with a speed governor so that the speed of the generator is practically constant. Under such condition, the generator performance deals primarily with the relation between excitation, terminal voltage and load. These relations can be best exhibited graphically by means of curves known as generator characteristics. These characteristics show at a glance the behaviour of the generator under different load conditions.

D.C. Generator Characteristics The following are the three most important characteristics of a d.c. generator:

1. Open Circuit Characteristic (O.C.C.):

This curve shows the relation between the generated e.m.f. at no-load (E0) and the field current (If) at constant speed. It is also known as magnetic characteristic or no-load saturation curve. Its shape is practically the same for all generators whether separately or self-excited. The data for O.C.C. curve are obtained experimentally by operating the generator at no load and constant speed and recording the change in terminal voltage as the field current is varied.

2. Internal or Total characteristic (E/Ia)

This curve shows the relation between the generated e.m.f. on load (E) and the armature current (Ia). The e.m.f. E is less than E0 due to the demagnetizing effect of armature reaction. Therefore, this curve will lie below the open circuit characteristic (O.C.C.). The internal characteristic is of interest chiefly to the designer. It cannot be obtained directly by experiment. It is because a voltmeter cannot read the e.m.f. generated on load due to the voltage drop in armature resistance.

The internal characteristic can be obtained from external characteristic if winding resistances are known because armature reaction effect is included in both characteristics

3. External characteristic (V/IL):

This curve shows the relation between the terminal voltage (V) and load current (IL). The terminal voltage V will be less than E due to voltage drop in the armature circuit. Therefore, this curve will lie below the internal characteristic. This characteristic is very important in determining the suitability of a generator for a given purpose. It can be obtained by making simultaneous measurements of terminal voltage and load current (with voltmeter and ammeter) of a loaded generator.

UNIT-III

Ignition Systems

Ignition System

In spark ignition engines, a device is required to ignite the compressed air-fuel mixture at the end of compression stroke. Ignition system fulfills this requirement. It is a part of electrical system which carries the electric current at required voltage to the spark plug which generates spark at correct time. It consists of a battery, switch, distributor ignition coil, spark plugs and necessary wiring.

A compression ignition engine, i.e. a diesel engine does not require any ignition system. Because, self ignition of fuel air mixture takes place when diesel is injected in the compressed air at high temperature at the end of compression stroke.

Requirements Of An Ignition System

(a) The ignition system should be capable of producing high voltage current, as high as 25000 volts, so that spark plug can produce spark across its electrode gap.

(b) It should produce spark for sufficient duration so that mixture can be ignited at all operating speeds of automobile.

(c) Ignition system should function satisfactory at all engine speeds.

(d) Longer life of contact points and spark plug.

(e) Spark must generate at correct time at the end of compression stroke in every cycle of engine operation.

(f) The system must be easy to maintain, light in weight and compact in size.

(g) There should be provision of spark advance with speed and load.

(h) It should be able to function smoothly even when the spark plug electrodes are deposited with carbon lead or oil.

Types Of Ignition Systems

There are three types of ignition systems which are used in petrol engines.

(a) Battery ignition system or coil ignition system.

(b) Magneto ignition system.

(c) Electronic ignition system.

In battery ignition system, the current in the primary winding is supplied by a battery whereas it is supplied by a magneto in magneto ignition system.

Battery ignition system is used in cars and light truck. Magneto ignition system is used in some scooters. Both the systems work on the principle of mutual electromagnetic induction. Electronic ignition systems use solid state devices such as transistors and capacitors.

Battery or Coil Ignition System

Battery ignition system consists of a battery of 6 or 12 volts, ignition switch, induction coil, contact breaker, condenser, distributor and spark plugs. A typical battery ignition system for four cylinder SI engine has been shown in Figure

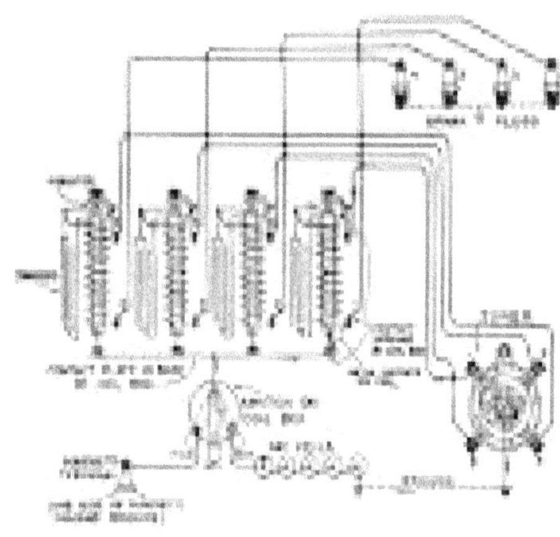

Battery or Coil Ignition System

The primary circuit consists of battery, switch, primary winding and contact breaker point which is grounded. A condenser is also connected in parallel to the contact breaker points. One end of the condenser is grounded and other connected to the contact breaker arm. It is provided to avoid sparking at contact breaker points so as to increase their life.

The secondary ignition circuit consists of secondary winding distributors and spark plugs. All spark plugs are grounded.

The ignition coil steps up 12 volts (or 6 volt) supply to a very high voltage which may range from 20,000 to 30,000 volts. A high voltage is required for the spark to jump across the spark plug gas. This spark ignites the air-fuel mixture as the end of compression stroke. The rotor of the distributor revolves and distributors the current to the four segments which send the current to different spark plugs. For a 4-cylinder engine the cam of the contact breaker has four lobes. Therefore, it makes and breaks the contact of the primary circuit four times in every revolution of cam. Because of which current is distributed to all the spark plugs in some definite sequence.

The primary winding of ignition coil has less number of turns (e.g. 200 turns) of thick wire. The secondary winding has relatively large number of turns (e.g. 20,000 turns) of thin wire. When ignition switch in turned on, the current flows from battery to the primary winding. This produces magnetic field in the coil. When the contact point is open, the magnetic field collapses and the movement of the magnetic field induces current in the secondary winding of ignition coil. As the number of turns in secondary winding are more, a very high voltage is produced across the terminals of secondary.

The distributor sends this high voltage to the proper spark plug which generates spark for ignition of fuel-air mixture. In this way, high voltage current is passed to all spark in a definite order so that combustion of fuel-air mixture takes place in all cylinders of the engine.

A ballast register is connected in series in primary circuit to regulate the current. At the time of starting this register is bypassed so that more current can flow in this circuit. The breaker points are held by a spring except when they are forced apart by lobes of the cam

. **Advantages**

(a) Low initial cost.

(b) Better spark at low speeds and better starting than magneto system.

(c) Reliable system.

(d) No problems due to adjustment of spark timings.

(e) Simpler than magneto system.

Disadvantages

(a) Battery requires periodical maintenance.

(b) In case of battery malfunction, engine cannot be started.

Magneto-ignition System

This system consists of a magneto in place of a battery. So, the magneto produces and supplies current in primary winding. Rest of the system is same as that in battery ignition system. A magneto ignition system for a four cylinder SI engine has been shown in Figure .

The magneto consists of a fixed armature having primary and secondary windings and a rotating magnetic assembly. This rotating assembly is driven by the engine.

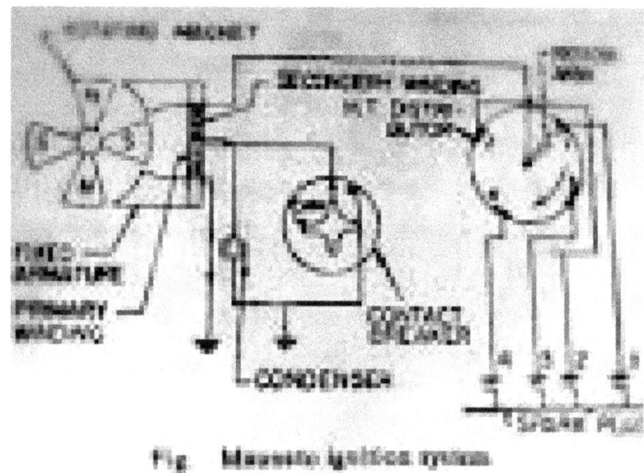

Magneto Ignition System

Rotation of magneto generates current in primary winding having small number of turns. Secondary winding having large number of turns generates high voltage current which is supplied to distributor. The distributor sends this current to respective spark plugs. The magneto may be of rotating armature type or rotating magnet type. In rotating armature type magneto, the armature having primary and secondary windings and the condenser rotates between the poles of a stationary horse shoe magnet. In magneto, the magnetic field is produced by permanent magnets.

Advantages

(a) Better reliability due to absence of battery and low maintenance.

(b) Better suited for medium and high speed engines.

(c) Modern magneto systems are more compact, therefore require less space.

Disadvantages

(a) Adjustment of spark timings adversely affects the voltage.

(b) Burning of electrodes is possible at high engine speeds due to high voltage.

(c) Cost is more than that of magneto ignition systems.

FUNCTIONS OF COMPONENTS USED IN CIRCUITS

Functions of various components used in battery (coil) ignition and magneto-ignition systems are discussed here in brief.

Battery

It is an important component of electrical system. The battery supplies the necessary current to the primary winding of ignition coil which is converted into high voltage current to produce spark. It also supplied current to run the starting motor when engine is cranked for starting. A battery stores energy in the form of chemical energy and supplies it for running lights and other accessories of an automobile. Lead-acid battery is commonly used in most of the automobiles.

Ignition or Induction Coil

The ignition coil is step up transformer to increase the voltage form 12 volt or 6 volt to 20000-30000 volts. It consists of a primary winding and a secondary winding wound on a laminated soft iron core. Primary winding contains about 300 turns made of thick wire. Secondary consists of about 20000 turns of thin wire. In a can type coil, secondary is wound on the soft core over which primary is wound. This assembly is housed in a steel casing fitted with a cap. The cap is made of insulating material. The terminals for electrical connections are provided in cap. To save the windings from moisture and to improve insulation, windings are dipped in oil.

Contact Breakers

Contact breaker is required to make contact and break contact of the primary circuit of ignition system. It consists of two contact breaker points as shown in Figures. One point remains fixed while the other can move. A cam is sued to move the movable point. As cam moves, the contact is made and broken alternately. Primary circuit breaks when the breaker points open. Magnetic field collapses due to this. This produces high voltage current in the secondary winding which is supplied to the distributor. This current is distributor to proper spark plug where it produces spark for ignition of fuel-air mixture.

Condenser

The function of the condenser in the ignition system is to absorb and store the inductive current generated in the coil. If condenser is not provided, the induced current will cause arcing at the breaker points. This will cause burning of the breaker points.

Distributor

The distributor sends the high voltage current, generated in the secondary winding, to the proper spark plug at proper time. If the automobile is having a four cylinder engine, it will have four spark plugs.

The cap of the distributor is connected to the secondary winding of coil. It has a rotor which rotates and comes in contact with the terminals (4 in number for 4 spark plugs) placed around the rotor. As the rotor comes in contact with the terminals (numbered 1, 2, 3 and 4 in Figures), the current is passed to the respective spark plug at proper time when spark is needed.

Ignition Switch

The function of the ignition switch is to connect the battery and starting motor in the automobiles having self starting system.

Example : In car, jeep, etc.

Its function is to connect battery to induction coil in the battery ignition system.

Spark Plugs

The function of the spark plug is to produce spark between its electrodes. This spark is used to ignite the fuel-air mixture in the spark ignition (SI) engines.

Magneto

Magneto is used in magneto ignition system. Magneto is a kind of generator to provide electrical energy to run the ignition system. It is replacement of battery for ignition. When it is rotated by the engine, it produces high voltage current to be supplied to spark plugs through the distributor.

Ignition Advance

The purpose of spark advance mechanism is to assure that under every condition of engine operation, ignition takes place at the most favorable instant in time i.e. most favorable from a standpoint of engine power, fuel economy and minimum exhaust dilution. By means of these mechanisms the advance angle is accurately set so that ignition occurs before TDC point of the piston. The engine speed and the engine load are the control quantities required for the automatic adjustment of the ignition timing. Most of the engines are fitted with mechanisms which are integral with the distributor and automatically regulate the optimum spark advance to account for change of speed and load. The two mechanisms used are:

    (a) Centrifugal advance mechanism, and

    (b) Vacuum advance mechanism.

Centrifugal Advance Mechanism

    The centrifugal advance mechanism controls the ignition timing for full- load operation. The adjustment mechanism is designed so that its operation results in the desired advance of the spark. The cam is mounted, movably, on the distributor shaft so that as the speed increases, the flyweights which are swung farther and farther outward, shaft the cam in the direction of shaft rotation. As a result, the cam lobes make contact with the breaker lever rubbing block somewhat earlier, thus shifting the ignition point in the early or advance direction.

Depending on the speed of the engine, and therefore of the shaft, the weights are swung outward a greater or a lesser distance from the center. They are then held in the extended position, in a state of equilibrium corresponding to the shifted timing angle, by a retaining

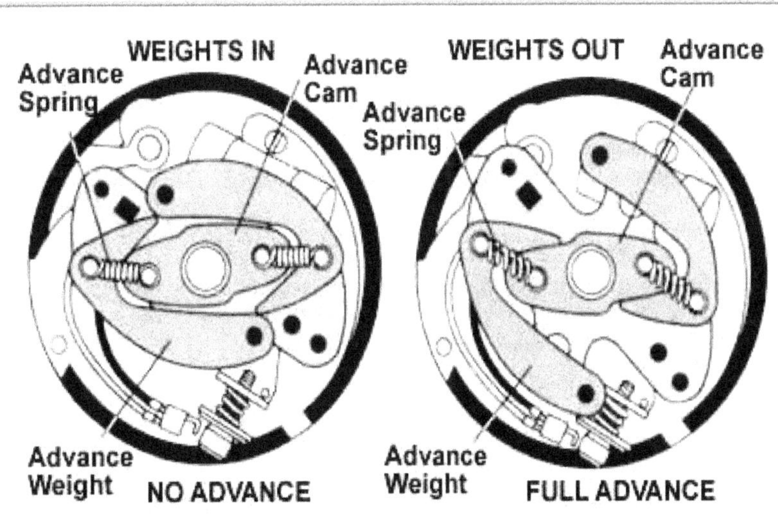

spring which exactly balances the centrifugal force. The weights shift the cam either or a rolling contact or sliding contact basis; for this reasons we distinguish between the rolling contact type and the sliding contact type of centrifugal advance mechanism.

The beginning of the timing adjustment in the range of low engine speeds and the continues adjustment based on the full load curve are determined by the size of the weights by the shape of the contact mechanisms (rolling or sliding contact type), and by the retaining springs, all of which can be widely differing designs. The centrifugal force controlled cam is fitted with a lower limit stop for purposes of setting the beginning of the adjustment, and also with an upper limit stop to restrict the greatest possible full load adjustment.

Vacuum Advance Mechanism

Vacuum advance mechanism shifts the ignition point under partial load operation. The adjustment system is designed so that its operation results in the prescribed partial load advance curve. In this mechanism the adjustment control quantity is the static vacuum prevailing in the carburetor, a pressure which depends on the position of the throttle valve at any given time and which is at a maximum when this valve is about half open. This explains the vacuum maximum.

The diaphragm of a vacuum unit is moved by changes in gas pressure. The position of this diaphragm is determined by the pressure differential at any given moment between the prevailing vacuum and atmospheric pressure. The beginning of adjustment is set by the pre-established tension on a compression spring. The diaphragm area, the spring force, and the spring rigidity are all selected in accordance with the partial –load advance curve which is to be followed and are all balanced with respect to each other. The diaphragm movement is transmitted through a vacuum advance arm connected to the movable breaker plate, and this movement shifts the breaker plate an additional amount under partial load Ignition Systems condition in a direction opposite to the direction of rotation of the distributor shaft. Limit stops on the vacuum advance arm in the base of the vacuum unit restrict the range of adjustment.

The vacuum advance mechanism operates independent of the centrifugal advance mechanism. The mechanical interplay between the two advance mechanisms, however, permits the total adjustment angle at any given time to be the result of the addition of the shifts provided by the two individual mechanisms operates in conjunction with the engine is operating under partial load.

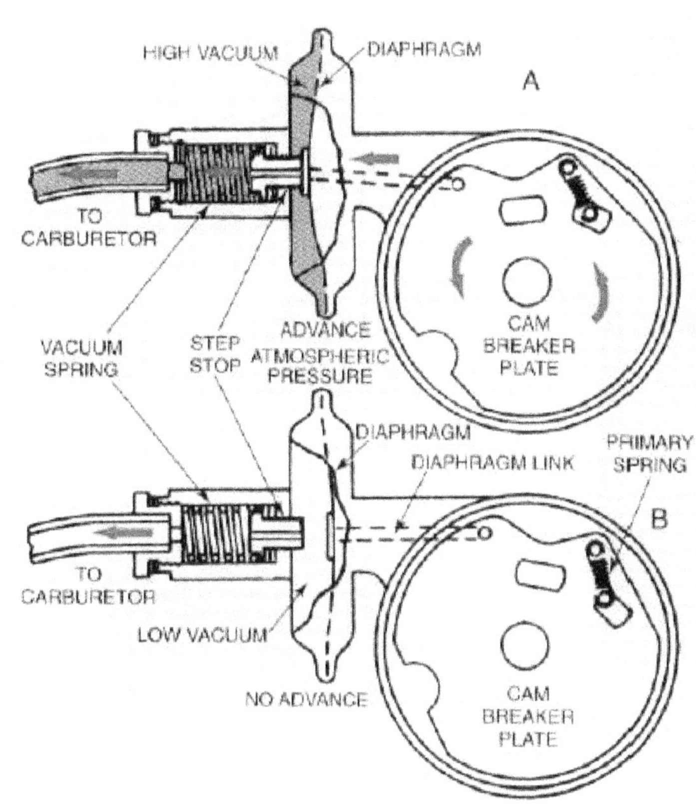

SPARK PLUGS

The simple requirement of a spark plug is that it must allow a spark to form within the combustion chamber, to initiate burning. In order to do this the plug has to withstand a number of severe conditions. Consider, as an example, a four-cylinder four-stroke engine with a compression ratio of 9:1, running at speeds up to 5000 rev/min. The following conditions are typical. At this speed the four-stroke cycle will repeat every 24 ms.

_ End of induction stroke –0.9 bar at 65 ° C.

_ Ignition firing point –9 bar at 350 ° C.

_ Highest value during power stroke –45 bar at 3000 ° C.

_ Power stroke completed –4 bar at 1100 ° C.

Besides the above conditions, the spark plug must withstand severe vibration and a harsh chemical environment. Finally, but perhaps most important, the insulation properties must withstand voltage pressures up to 40kV.

Construction

The centre electrode is connected to the top terminal by a stud. The electrode is constructed of a nickel-based alloy. Silver and platinum are also used for some applications. If a copper core is used in the electrode this improves the thermal conduction properties.

The insulating material is ceramic-based and of a very high grade. Aluminium oxide, Al2O3 (95% pure), is a popular choice, it is bonded into the metal parts and glazed on the outside surface. The properties of this material, which make it most suitable, are as follows:

_ Young's modulus: 340kN/mm2.

_ Coefficient of thermal expansion: 7.8 x10K^{-1}.

_ Thermal conductivity: 15–5W/mK (Range 200–900 ° C).

_ Electrical resistance: $10^{13}\Omega$/m.

The above list is intended as a guide only, as actual values can vary widely with slight manufacturing changes. The electrically conductive glass seal between the electrode and terminal stud is also used as a resistor. This resistor has two functions. First, to prevent burn-off of the centre electrode, and secondly to reduce radio interference. In both cases the desired effect is achieved because the resistor damps the current at the instant of ignition.

Flash-over, or tracking down the outside of the plug insulation, is prevented by ribs that effectively increase the surface distance from the terminal to the metal fixing bolt, which is of course earthed to the engine.

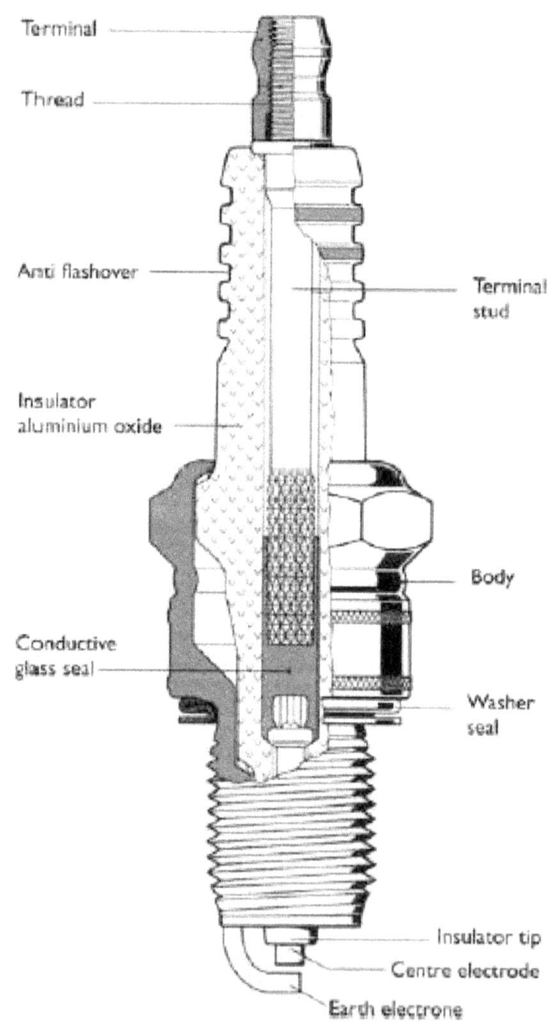

Electrode materials

The material chosen for the spark plug electrode must exhibit the following properties:

_ High thermal conductivity.

_ High corrosion resistance.

_ High resistance to burn-off.

For normal applications, alloys of nickel are used for the electrode material. Chromium, manganese, silicon and magnesium are examples of the alloying constituents. These alloys exhibit excellent properties with respect to corrosion and burn-off resistance.

To improve on the thermal conductivity, compound electrodes are used. These allow a greater nose projection for the same temperature range, as discussed in the last section. A common example of this type of plug is the copper-core spark plug.

Silver electrodes are used for specialist applications as silver has very good thermal and electrical properties. Again, with these plugs nose length can be increased within the same temperature range.

The thermal conductivity of some electrode materials is listed for comparison.

_ Silver 407 W/m K

_ Copper 384 W/m K

_ Platinum 70 W/m K

_ Nickel 59 W/m K

Compound electrodes have an average thermal conductivity of about 200 W/m K. Platinum tips are used for some spark plug applications due to the very high burn-off resistance of this material. It is also possible because of this to use much smaller diameter electrodes, thus increasing mixture accessibility. Platinum also has a catalytic effect, further accelerating the combustion process.

Electrode gap

Spark plug electrode gaps have, in general, increased as the power of the ignition systems driving the spark has increased. The simple relationship between plug gap and voltage required is that, as the gap increases so must the voltage (leaving aside engine operating conditions). Furthermore, the energy available to form a spark at a fixed engine speed is constant, which means that a larger gap using higher voltage will result in a shorter duration spark. A smaller gap will allow a longer duration spark. For cold starting an engine and for igniting weak mixtures, the duration of the spark is critical. Likewise the plug gap must be as large as possible to allow easy access for the mixture in order to prevent quenching of the flame.

The final choice is therefore a compromise reached through testing and development of a particular application. Plug gaps in the region of 0.6–1.2 mm seem to be the norm at present.

Electrical and Electronic Ignition Systems

Electronic Ignition System

Electronic ignition is now fitted to almost all spark ignition vehicles. This is because the conventional mechanical system has some major disadvantages.

● Mechanical problems with the contact breakers, not the least of which is the limited lifetime.

● Current flow in the primary circuit is limited to about 4 A or damage will occur to the contacts – or at least the lifetime will be seriously reduced.

● Legislation requires stringent emission limits, which means the ignition timing must stay in tune for a long period of time.

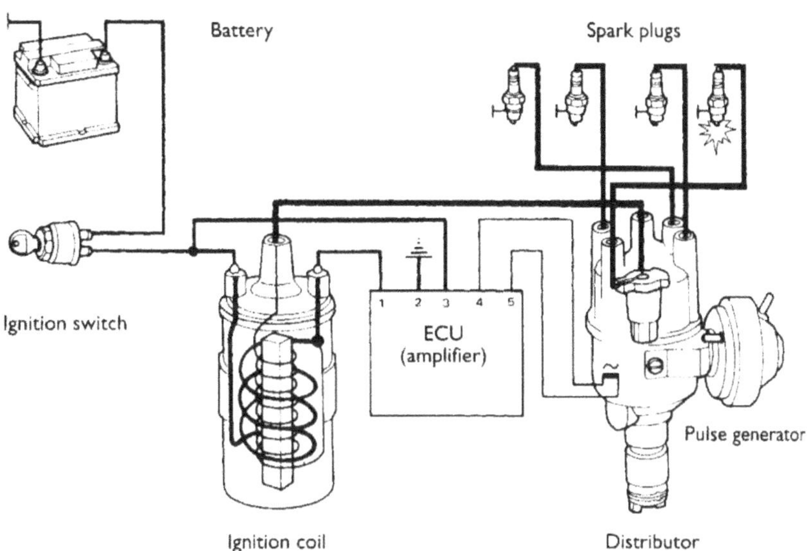

Electronic Ignition System

● Weaker mixtures require more energy from the spark to ensure successful ignition, even at very high engine speed.

These problems can be overcome by using a power transistor to carry out the switching function and a pulse generator to provide the timing signal. Very early forms of electronic ignition used the existing contact breakers as the signal provider. This was a step in the right direction but did not overcome all the mechanical limitations, such as contact bounce and timing slip. Most (all?) systems nowadays are constant energy, ensuring high performance ignition even at high engine speed. Figure the circuit of a standard electronic ignition system.

Distributorless Ignition

Distributorless ignition systems (DIS) have been around for almost a decade now, and have eliminated much of the maintenance that used to be associated with the ignition system. No distributor means there's no distributor cap or rotor to replace, and no troublesome vacuum or mechanical advance mechanisms to cause timing problems. Consequently, DIS ignition systems are pretty reliable.

Even so, that doesn't mean they are trouble-free. Failures can and do occur for a variety of reasons. So knowing how to identify and diagnose common DIS problems can save you a lot of guesswork the next time you encounter an engine that cranks but refuses to start, or one that runs but is missing or misfiring on one or more cylinders.

If an engine cranks but won't start, is it fuel, ignition or compression? Ignition is usually the easiest of the three to check because on most engines, all you have to do is pull off a plug wire and check for spark when the engine is cranked. On coil-over-plug DIS systems, there are no plug wires so you have to remove a coil and use a plug wire or adapter to check for a spark.

If there's no spark in one cylinder, try another. No spark in any cylinder would most likely indicate a failed DIS module or crankshaft position sensor. Many engines that are equipped with electronic fuel injection also use the crankshaft position sensor signal to trigger the fuel injectors. So, if there's no spark and no injector activity, the problem is likely in the crank position sensor. No spark in only one cylinder or two cylinders that share a coil would tell you a coil has probably failed.

Principle of Operation

Distributorless ignition system used extensively by Ford incorporates all the features of electronic spark advance systems, except a special type of ignition coil is used in place of HT distributor. The system is generally used only on four- or six-cylinder engines, because the control system becomes highly complex for higher number of cylinders. It works on the principle of the lost spark. The spark distribution is achieved by the help of two double ended coils, fired alternately by the ECU. The ignition timing is obtained from a crankshaft speed and position sensor as well as through load and other corrections. When one of the coils is fired, a spark is delivered to two engine cylinders, either 1 and 4, or 2 and 3. The spark delivered to the cylinder on the compression stroke ignites the mixture as normal. Whereas the spark in other cylinder causes no effect, as this cylinder is just completing its exhaust stroke. Because of the low compression and the exhaust gases in the lost spark cylinder, the voltage only of about 3 kV is needed for the spark to jump the gap. This is similar to cap voltage of the more conventional rotor arm. The spark produced in the compression cylinder is therefore not affected. It may be noted that the spark on one of the cylinders jumps from the earth electrode to the spark plug centre, whereas in others it jumps from the centre electrode. This is because the energy available from modern constant energy systems produces a spark of suitable quality in either direction. However, the disadvantage is that the spark plugs may wear more quickly with this system.

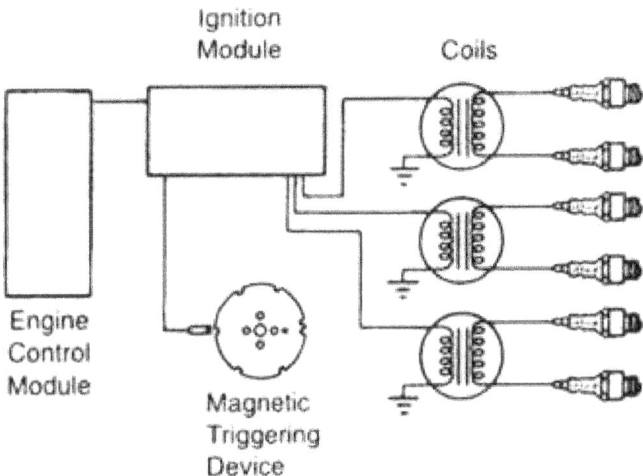

System Components

The distributorless ignition system contains three main components such as the electronic module, a crankshaft position sensor and the distributorless ignition coil. Many systems use a manifold absolute pressure sensor, integrated in the module. The module functions almost in the same way as the electronic spark advance system.

The crankshaft position sensor operates in the similar way to the one described in the previous section. It is also a reluctance sensor positioned against the front of the flywheel or against a reluctor wheel just behind the front crankshaft pulley. The tooth pattern uses 36-1 teeth, which are spaced at 10 degree intervals, with a gap for the 36th tooth. The missing tooth is located at 90 degrees before TDC for numbers 1 and 4 cylinders. This reference position is located a fixed number of degrees before TDC for calculating the timing or ignition point as a fixed angle after the reference mark.

The distributorless ignition coil (Fig. 16.56) has a low tension winding, which is supplied with battery voltage to a centre terminal. The appropriate half of the winding is then connected to earth in the module. The high tension windings are separate and are specific to cylinders 1 and 4, or 2 and 3. Figure 16.57 shows a typical Ford distributorless ignition coil. The Citroen 2 CV has been using a double ended ignition coil together with contact breakers for many years.

Fault Diagnosis

The distributorless ignition system is highly reliable, specifically because it does not have any moving parts. The normal manufacturers servicing schedule should be adhered to for the replacement of spark plugs (often after 19,200 km operation). Some problems may be faced when trying to examine HT oscilloscope patterns, due to the lack of a king lead. This can be overcome by using a special adapter and shifting the sensing clip to each lead in turn. An ohmmeter can be used to test the distributorless ignition coil. The resistance of each primary winding should be 0.5 Q and the secondary windings between 11 and 16 kQ. The coil produces open circuit voltage in excess of 37 kV. The plug leads have integral retaining clips to prevent water ingress and vibration problems. The maximum resistance for the HT leads is 30 kQ per lead. Except for the octane adjustment on some models no service adjustments are possible with this system. This adjustment involves connecting two pins together on the module for normal operation, or earthing one pin or the other to change to a different fuel. The actual procedure as specified by the manufacturer for each particular model should be followed.

DIGITAL IGNITION SYTEM

Electronic Ignition System is as follow :

(a) Capacitance Discharge Ignition system

(b) Transistorized system

(c) Piezo-electric Ignition system

(d) The Texaco Ignition system

Capacitance Discharge Ignition System

It mainly consists of 6-12 V battery, ignition switch, DC to DC convertor, charging resistance, tank capacitor, Silicon Controlled Rectifier (SCR), SCR-triggering device, step up transformer, spark plugs.

A 6-12 volt battery is connected to DC to DC converter i.e. power circuit through the ignition switch, which is designed to give or increase the voltage to 250-350 volts. This high voltage is used to charge the tank capacitor (or condenser) to this voltage through the charging resistance. The charging resistance is also so designed that it controls the required current in the

SCR.

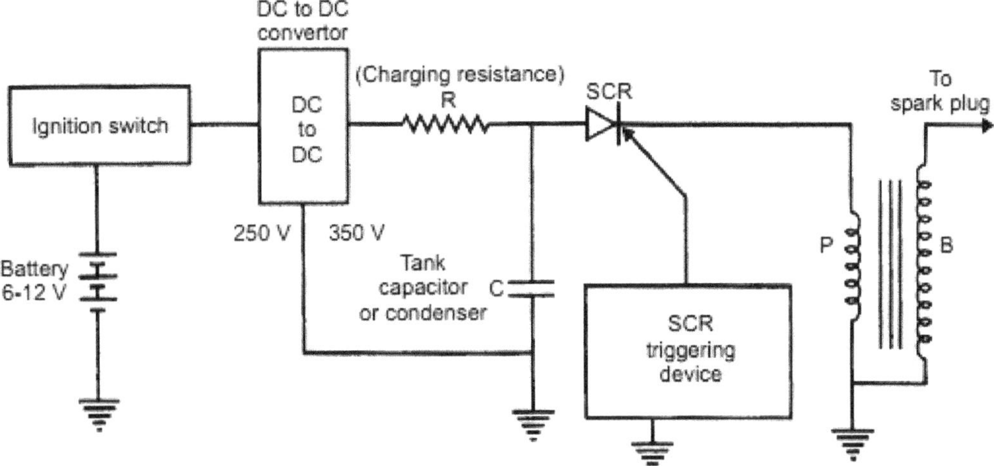

Figure 4.4 : Capacitance Discharge Ignition System

Depending upon the engine firing order, whenever the SCR triggering device, sends a pulse, then the current flowing through the primary winding is stopped. And the magnetic field begins to collapse. This collapsing magnetic field will induce or step up high voltage current in the secondary, which while jumping the spark plug gap produces the spark, and the charge of air fuel mixture is ignited.

Transistorized Assisted Contact (TAC) Ignition System

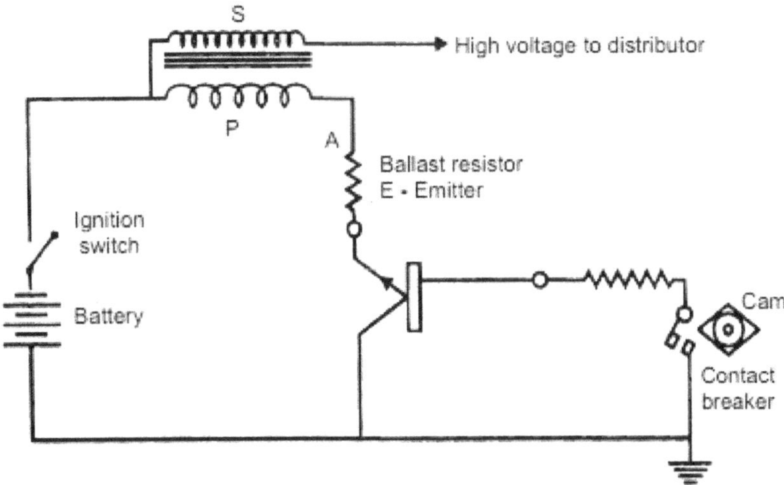

Advantages

(a) The low breaker-current ensures longer life.

(b) The smaller gap and lighter point assembly increase dwell time minimize contact bouncing and improve repeatability of secondary voltage.

(c) The low primary inductance reduces primary inductance reduces primary current drop-off at high speeds.

Disadvantages

(a) As in the conventional system, mechanical breaker points are necessary for timing the spark.

(b) The cost of the ignition system is increased.

(c) The voltage rise-time at the spark plug is about the same as before.

Piezo-electric Ignition System

The development of synthetic piezo-electric materials producing about 22 kV by mechanical loading of a small crystal resulted in some ignition systems for single cylinder engines. But due to difficulties of high mechanical loading need of the order of 500 kg timely control and ability to produce sufficient voltage, these systems have not been able to come up.

The Texaco Ignition System

Due to the increased emphasis on exhaust emission control, there has been a sudden interest in exhaust gas recirculation systems and lean fuel-air mixtures. To avoid the problems of burning of lean mixtures, the Texaco Ignition system has been developed. It provides a spark of controlled duration which means that the spark duration in crank angle degrees can be made constant at all engine speeds. It is a AC system. This system consists of three basic units, a power unit, a control unit and a distributor sensor. This system can give stable ignition up to A/F ratios as high as 24 : 1.

Non–Contact–type Ignition Triggering devices

Triggering is arranged so that the ignition coil is charged in sufficient time before the actual ignition point. This requires the formation of a dwell period (coil saturation time) in the ignition system. The energy to be released as a spark is usually stored in a coil as magnetic energy (with conventional systems). In other cases, this can be replaced with a capacitor as electrostatic energy, such as in a capacitive discharge ignition system (CDI), in which case the role of the coil changes to simply that of an energy transfer device. The high tension results from disconnecting the primary inductor from the power supply followed by transformation.

The high tension is then applied via the distributor to the cylinder currently performing the working stroke. All this combines to produce the required firing voltage, which is determined by the cylinder pressure, a byproduct of the inlet charge and compression, combined with the gap, temperature and shape of the spark plug electrode. The ignition system will then only deliver the voltage necessary to fire the spark plug. If all is well, the mixture will be successfully ignited. If insufficient energy is available, ignition does not occur, thus allowing a misfire. This is why adequate ignition must be provided.

Electronically–Assisted and Full Electronic Ignition System

The need for higher mileage, reduced emissions and greater reliability has led to the development of the electronic ignition systems. These systems generate a much stronger spark which is needed to ignite leaner fuel mixtures. Breaker point systems needed a resistor to reduce the operating voltage of the primary circuit in order to prolong the life of the points. The primary circuit of the electronic ignition systems operates on full battery voltage which helps to develop a stronger spark. Spark plug gaps have widened due to the ability of the increased voltage to jump the larger gap. Cleaner combustion and less deposit have led to longer spark plug life.
On some systems, the ignition coil has been moved inside the distributor cap. This system is said to have an internal coil as opposed to the conventional external one.

Electronic Ignition systems are not as complicated as they may first appear. In fact, they differ only slightly from conventional point ignition systems. Like conventional ignition systems, electronic systems have two circuits: a primary circuit and a secondary circuit. The entire secondary circuit is the same as in a conventional ignition system. In addition, the section of the primary circuit from the battery to the battery terminal at the coil is the same as in a conventional ignition system.

Electronic ignition systems differ from conventional ignition systems in the distributor component area. Instead of a distributor cam, breaker plate, points, and condenser, an electronic ignition system has an armature (called by various names such as a trigger wheel, reluctor, etc.), a pickup coil (stator, sensor, etc.), and an electronic control module.
Essentially, all electronic ignition systems operate in the following manner: With the ignition switch turned on, primary (battery) current flows from the battery through the ignition switch to the coil primary windings. Primary current is turned on and off by the action of the armature as it revolves past the pickup coil or sensor. As each tooth of the armature nears the pickup coil, it

creates a voltage that signals the electronic mod

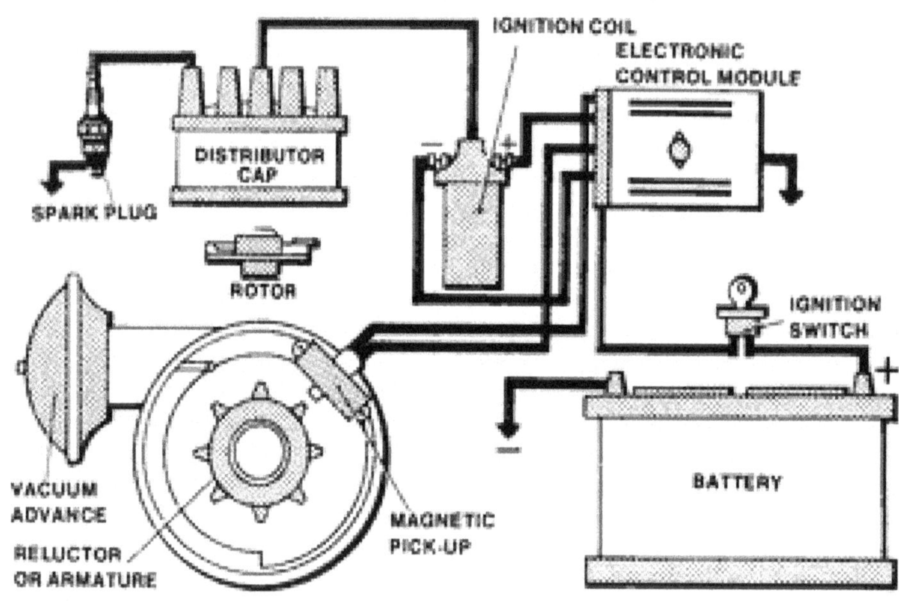

ule to turn off the coil primary current. A timing circuit in the module will turn the current on again after the coil field has collapsed. When the current is off, however, the magnetic field built up in the coil is allowed to collapse, which causes a high voltage in the secondary windings of the coil. It is now operating on the secondary ignition circuit, which is the same as in a conventional ignition system.

Troubleshooting electronic ignition systems ordinarily requires the use of a voltmeter and/or an ohmmeter. Sometimes the use of an ammeter is also required. Because of differences in design and construction, troubleshooting is specific to each system. A complete troubleshooting guide for you particular application can be found in the Chilton's Total Car Care manual.

Unit-5

Wiring, Lighting and Other Instruments and Sensors

AUTOMOTIVE WIRING

Electrical power and control signals must be delivered to electrical devices reliably and safely so that the electrical system functions are not impaired or converted to hazards. To fulfill power distribution military vehicles, use one-and two-wire circuits, wiring harnesses, and terminal connections.

Among your many duties will be the job of maintaining and repairing automotive electrical systems. All vehicles are not wired in exactly the same manner; however, once you understand the circuit of one vehicle, you should be able to trace an electrical circuit of any vehicle using wiring diagrams and color codes.

ONE-AND TWO-WIRE CIRCUITS

Tracing wiring circuits, particularly those connecting lights or warning and signal devices, is no simple task. The branch circuits making up the individual systems have one wire to conduct electricity from the battery to the unit requiring it and ground connections at the battery and the unit to complete the circuit. These are called ONE-WIRE CIRCUITS or branches of a GROUND RETURN SYSTEM. In automotive electrical systems with branch circuits that lead to all parts of the equipment, the ground return system saves installation time and eliminates the need for an additional wiring to complete the circuit. The all-metal construction of the automotive equipment makes it possible to use this system.

The TWO-WIRE CIRCUIT requires two wires to complete the electrical circuit- one wire from the source of electrical energy to the unit it will operate, and another wire to complete the circuit from the unit back to the source of the electrical power. Two-wire circuits provide positive connection for light and electrical brakes on some trailers. The coupling between the trailer and the equipment, although made of metal and a conductor of electricity, has to be jointed to move freely. The rather loose joint or coupling does not provide the positive and continuous connection required to use a ground return system between two vehicles. The two-wire circuit is commonly used on equipment subject to frequent or heavy vibrations. Tracked equipment, off-road vehicles (tactical), and many types of construction equipment are wired in this manner.

Insulated Return

Some vehicle application requires a separate insulated-cable system for both the feed and the return conductors. It is also safer because with separate feed and return cables, it is practically impossible for the cable conductors to short even if chafed and touching any of the metal bodywork, as the body is not live since it is not a part of the electrical circuits. From the safety reasons, an insulated return is essential for vehicles transporting highly flammable liquids and gases, where a spark could very easily set off an explosion or a fire. The vehicles, such as coaches and double-decker buses use large quantity of plastic panelling. For these vehicles an insulated return is more reliable and safer. The insulated return off course uses extra cable that makes the overall wiring harness heavier, less flexible, and bulky, consequently increases the cost to some extent.

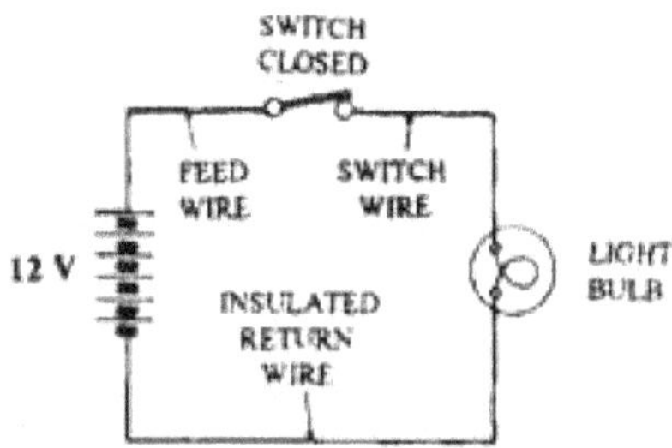

Earth Return.

All electrical circuits incorporate both a feed and a return conductor between the battery and the component requiring supply of electrical energy. The vehicle with a metal structure can be used as one of the two conducting paths. This is called as the earth return (Fig. 13.51). A live feed wire cable forms the other conductor. To complete the earth-return path, one end of a short thick cable is bolted to the chassis structure while the other end is attached to one of the battery terminal posts. The electrical component is also required to be earthed in a similar way. Only one battery-to-chassis conductor is necessary for a complete vehicle's wiring system and similarly any number of separate earth-return circuits can be wired. An earth-return system, therefore, reduces and simplifies the amount of wiring so that it is easy to trace electrical faults.

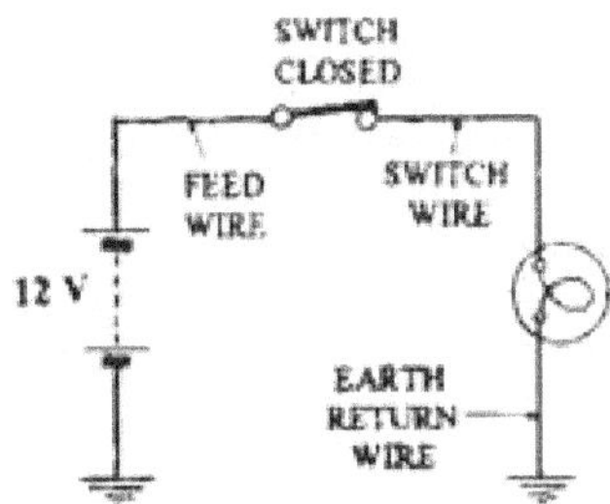

Positive and Negative earthing

In the beginning, it was the general practice of earthing the negative terminal of the battery, whereas the positive current was supplied to the electrical units. The negative earthing system is still used in the cars of American make.

In some countries, the negative earth system has been replaced by the positive earth system. This is because the positive earth system possesses certain advantages over the negative earth system. These advantages concern the temperature of the central spark plug electrode and the corrosion of some parts, it is well known fact that the positive terminal of the leadacid battery is attacked by the liberated gases. If this is the live terminal and the negative terminal earthed, the exposed part of the positive will become corroded.

Further it is also a well known fact that the positive point of the spark plug wears away more quickly than the negative point. In view of this fact, the central electrode of the plug will wear away quickly if made electrode of the plug will wear away quickly if made positive when compared with the metal electrode of the shell. Alternatively, the central electrode of the plug will have much longer life if made negative by earthing the positive terminal of the battery.

Another factor which plays an important role in the voltage requirements of a spark plug is the temperature of the negative electrode. The hotter this electrode is, the lower will be the voltage required for producing the spark, It has also been observed that more uniform voltages at the sparking points have been obtained with the central electrode being negative. Further, the metal rotor arm of the distributor, if made negative, will wear at a slower rate than if it were made positive.

There is an additional advantage of the positive earth method in the ignition coil elements the primary circuit voltage is added to the secondary circuit voltage, making it more economical.

Recently, with the adoption of alternators in place of generators, it has been observed that employing negative earth method is advantageous along with an ac current rectifier having transistors and diodes. This has meant shifting back to the negative earth method. However it is worth mentioning that the important advantages of the positive earth for the ignition system still hold good.

LIGHTING

The lighting circuit includes the battery, vehicle frame, all the lights, and various switches that control their use. The lighting circuit is known as a single-wire system since it uses the vehicle frame for the return.

The complete lighting circuit of a vehicle can be broken down into individual circuits, each having one or more lights and switches. In each separate circuit, the lights are connected in parallel, and the controlling switch is in series between the group of lights and the battery.

The marker lights, for example, are connected in parallel and are controlled by a single switch. In some installations, one switch controls the connections to the battery, while a selector switch determines which of two circuits is energized. The headlights, with their high and low beams, are an example of this type of circuit.

In some instances, such as the courtesy lights, several switches may be connected in parallel so that any switch may be used to turn on the light. When a wiring diagram is being studied, all light circuits can be traced from the battery through the ammeter to the switch (or switches) to the individual light.

LAMPS

Small gas-filled incandescent lamps with tungsten filaments are used on automotive and construction equipment. The filaments supply the light when sufficient current is flowing through them. They are designed to operate on a low voltage current of 12 or 24 volts, depending upon the voltage of the the vehicle will be of the single-or double-contact small one-half-candlepower bulbs to large 50- candlepower bulbs. The greater the candlepower of the lamp, the more current it requires when lighted. Lamps are identified by a number on the base. When you replace a lamp in a vehicle, be sure the new lamp is of the proper rating. The lamps within Lamps are rated as to size by the candlepower (luminous intensity) they produce. They range from types with nibs to fit bayonet sockets, as shown in lamp is also whiter than a conventional lamp, which increases lighting ability.

HEADLIGHTS

The headlights are sealed beam lamps that illuminate the road during nighttime operation. Headlights consist of a lens, one or two elements, and a integral reflector. When current flows through the element, the element gets white hot and glows. The reflector and lens direct the light forward.

Many modern passenger vehicles use halogen headlights. A halogen headlight contains a small, inner halogen lamp surrounded by a conventional sealed housing. A halogen headlamp increases light output by 25 percent with no increase in current. The halogen The headlight switch is an ON/ OFF switch and rheostat (variable resistor) in the dash panel) or on the steering column. The headlight switch controls current flow to the lamps of the headlight system. The rheostat is for adjusting the brightness of the instrument panel lights.

Military vehicles that are used in tactical situations are equipped with a headlight switch that is integrated with the blackout lighting switch. An important feature of this switch is that it reduces the possibility of accidentally turning on the lights in a blackout.

With no lights on, the main switch can be turned to the left without operating the mechanical switch to get blackout marker lights (including blackout taillights and stoplights) and blackout driving lights. But for stoplights for daylight driving or headlights for ordinary night driving, you must first lift the mechanical switch lever and then turn the main switch to the right. The auxiliary switch gives panel lights when the main switch is in any of its ON positions. But it will give parking lights only when the main switch is in service drive (to the extreme right). When the main switch is off, the auxiliary switch should not be moved from the OFF position.

DIMMER SWITCH

The dimmer switch controls the high and low headlamp beam function and is normally mounted on the floorboard or steering column. When the operator activates the dimmer switch, it changes the electrical connection to the headlights.

In one position, the high beams are turned on, and, in the other position, the dimmer changes them to low beam.

Aiming Headlights

The headlights can be aimed using a mechanical aimer or a wall screen. Either method assures that the headlight beams point in the direction specified by the vehicle manufacturer. Headlights that are aimed too high can blind oncoming vehicles. Headlights that are aimed too low or to one side will reduce the operator's visibility.

TURN-SIGNAL SYSTEMS

Vehicles that operate on any public road must be equipped with turn signals. These signals indicate a left or right turn by providing a flashing light signal at the rear and front of the vehicle.

The turn-signal switch is located on the steering column. It is designed to shut off automatically after the turn is completed by the action of the canceling cam. A common design for a turn-signal system is to use the same rear light for both the stop and turn signals. This somewhat complicates the design of the switch in that the stoplight circuit must pass through the turn-signal switch. When the turn-signal switch is turned off, it must pass stoplight current to the rear lights. As a left or right turn signal is selected, the stoplight circuit is open and the turn-signal circuit is closed to the respective rear light.

The turn signal flasher unit creates the flashing of the turn signal lights. It consists basically of a bimetallic (two dissimilar metals bonded together) strip wrapped in a wire coil. The bimetallic strip serves as one of the contact points.

When the turn signals are actuated, current flows into the flasher- first through the heating coil to the bimetallic strip, then through the contact points, then out of the flasher, where the circuit is completed through the turn-signal light. This sequence of events will repeat a few times a second, causing a steady flashing of the turn signals.

Electrical and Electronic Fuel Lift Pumps

In many modern cars the fuel pump is usually electric and located inside the fuel tank. The pump creates positive pressure in the fuel lines, pushing the gasoline to the engine. The higher gasoline pressure raises the boiling point. Placing the pump in the tank puts the component least likely to handle gasoline vapor well (the pump itself) farthest from the engine, submersed in cool liquid. Another benefit to placing the pump inside the tank is that it is less likely to start a fire. Though electrical components (such as a fuel pump) can spark and ignite fuel vapors, liquid fuel will not explode (see flammability limit) and therefore submerging the pump in the tank is one of the safest places to put it. In most cars, the fuel pump delivers a constant flow of gasoline to the engine; fuel not used is returned to the tank. This further reduces the chance of the fuel boiling, since it is never kept close to the hot engine for too long.

The ignition switch does not carry the power to the fuel pump; instead, it activates a relay which will handle the higher current load. It is common for the fuel pump relay to become oxidized and cease functioning; this is much more common than the actual fuel pump failing. Modern engines utilize solid-state control which allows the fuel pressure to be controlled via pulse-width modulation of the pump voltage. This increases the life of the pump, allows a smaller and lighter device to be used, and reduces electrical load.

Cars with electronic fuel injection have an electronic control unit (ECU) and this may be programmed with safety logic that will shut the electric fuel pump off, even if the engine is running. In the event of a collision this will prevent fuel leaking from any ruptured fuel line. Additionally, cars may have an inertia switch (usually located underneath the front passenger seat) that is "tripped" in the event of an impact, or a roll-over valve that will shut off the fuel pump in case the car rolls over.

Some ECUs may also be programmed to shut off the fuel pump if they detect low or zero oil pressure, for instance if the engine has suffered a terminal failure (with the subsequent risk of fire in the engine compartment).

The fuel sending unit assembly may be a combination of the electric fuel pump, the filter, the strainer, and the electronic device used to measure the amount of fuel in the tank via a float attached to a sensor which sends data to the dash-mounted fuel gauge. The fuel pump by itself is a relatively inexpensive part. But a mechanic at a garage might have a preference to install the entire unit assembly.

Fuel Level Indicator

Most fuel gauges are operated electrically and are composed of two units- the gauge, mounted on the instrument panel; and the sending unit, mounted in the fuel tank. The ignition switch is included in the fuel gauge circuit, so the gauge operates only when the ignition switch is in the ON position. Operation of the electrical gauge depends on either coil action or thermostatic action. The four types of fuel gauges are as follows:

The THERMOSTATIC FUEL GAUGE, SELF-REGULATING contains an electrically heated bimetallic strip that is linked to a pointer. A bimetallic strip consists of two dissimilar metals that, when heated, expand at different rates, causing it to deflect or bend. In the case of this gauge, the deflection of the bimetallic strip results in the movement of the pointer, causing the gauge to give a reading. The sending unit consists of a hinged arm with a float on the end. The movement of the arm controls a grounded point that makes contact with another point which is attached to an electrically heated bimetallic strip. The heating coils in the tank and the gauge are connected to each other in series.

The THERMOSTATIC FUEL GAUGE, EXTERNALLY REGULATED differs from a self-regulating system in the use of a variable resistance fuel tank sending unit and an external voltage-limiting device. The sending unit controls the gauge through the use of a rheostat (wire wound resistance unit whose value varies with its effective length). The effective length of the rheostat is controlled in the sending unit by a sliding brush that is operated by the float arm. The power supply to the gauge is kept constant through the use of a voltage limiter. The voltage limiter consists of a set of contact points that are controlled by an electrically heated bimetallic arm.

The THERMOSTATIC FUEL GAUGE, DIFFERENTIAL TYPE is similar to the other type of thermostatic fuel gauges, except that it uses two electrically heated bimetallic strips that share equally in operating and supporting the gauge pointer. The pointer position is obtained by dividing the available voltage between the two strips (differential). The tank unit is a rheostat type similar to that already described; however, it contains a wire-wound resistor that is connected between external terminals of one of the gauges of the bimetallic strip. The float arm moves a grounded brush that raises resistance progressively to one terminal, while lowering resistance to the other. This action causes the voltage division and resulting heat differential to the gauge strips formulating the gauge reading.

The MAGNETIC FUEL GAUGE consists of a pointer mounted on an armature. Depending upon the design, the armature may contain one or two poles. The gauge is motivated by a magnetic field that is created by two separate magnetic coils that are contained in the gauge. One of these coils is connected directly to the battery, producing a constant magnetic field. The other coil produces a variable field, whose strength is determined by a rheostat-type tank unit. The coils are placed 90 degrees apart.

Pressure Gauge

A pressure gauge is used widely in automotive and construction applications to keep track of such things as oil pressure, fuel line pressure, air brake system pressure, and the pressure in the hydraulic systems. Depending on the equipment, a mechanical gauge, an electrical gauge, or an indicator lamp may be used.

TEMPERATURE GAUGE

The temperature gauge is a very important indicator in construction and automotive equipment. The most common uses are to indicate engine coolant, transmission, differential oil, and hydraulic system temperature. Depending on the type of equipment, the gauge may be mechanical, electric, or a warning light.

The ELECTRIC GAUGE may be the thermostatic or magnetic type, as described previously. The sending unit (fig. 2-83) that is used varies, depending upon application.

1. The sending unit that is used with the thermostatic gauge consists of two bimetallic strips, each having a contact point. One bimetallic strip is heated electrically. The other strip bends to increase the tension of the contact points. The different positions of the bimetallic strip create the gauge readings.

2. The sending unit that is used with the magnetic gauge contains a device called a thermistor. A thermistor is an electronic device whose resistance decreases proportionally with an increase in temperature.

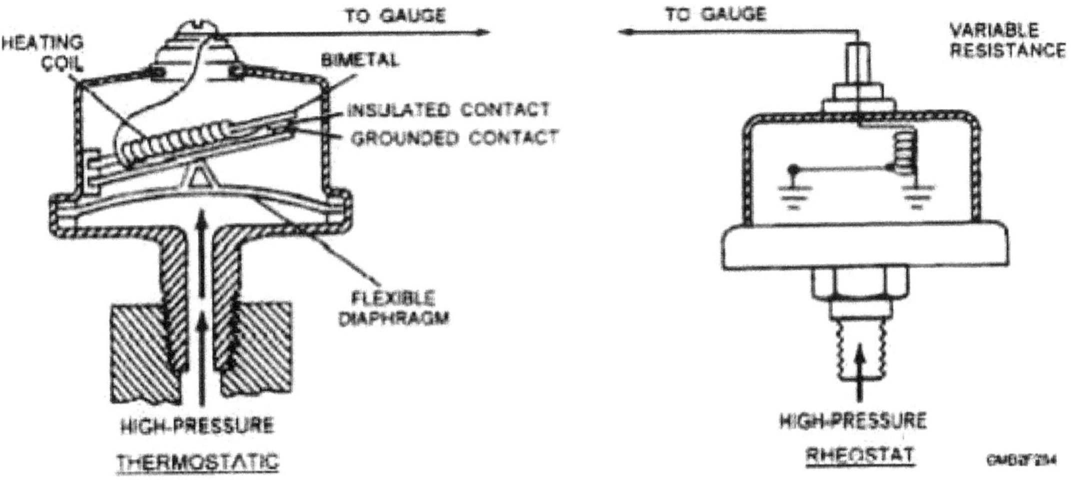

Figure 2-82.- Types of sending units for pressure gauges.

Figure 2-83.- Types of temperature gauge sending units.

SPEEDOMETER AND ODOMETERS

Mechanical Speedometers And Odometers

Both the mechanical speedometer and the tachometer consist of a permanent magnet that is rotated by a flexible shaft. Surrounding the rotating magnet is a metal cup that is attached to the indicating needle. The revolving magnetic field exerts a pull on the cup that forces it to rotate. The rotation of the cup is countered by a calibrated hairspring.

The influence of the hairspring and the rotating magnetic field on the cup produces accurate readings by the attached needle. The flexible shaft consists of a flexible outer casing that is made of either steel or plastic and an inner drive core that is made of wire-wound spring steel. Both ends of the core are molded square, so they can fit into the driving member at one end and the driven member at the other end and can transmit torque.

Gears on the transmission output shaft turn the flexible shaft that drives the speedometer. This shaft is referred to as the speedometer cable. A gear on the ignition distributor shaft turns the flexible shaft that drives the tachometer. This shaft is referred to as the tachometer cable.

The odometer of the mechanical speedometer is driven by a series of gears that originate at a spiral gear on the input shaft. The odometer consists of a series of drums with digits printed on the outer circumference that range from zero to nine. The drums are geared to each other so that each time the one furthest to the right makes one revolution, it will cause the one to its immediate left to advance one digit. The second to the right then will advance the drum to its immediate left one digit for every revolution it makes. This sequence continues to the left through the entire series of drums. The odometer usually contains six digits to record 99,999.9 miles or kilometers. However, models with trip odometers do not record tenths, thereby contain only five digits. When the odometer reaches its highest value, it will automatically reset to zero. Newer vehicles incorporate a small dye pad in the odometer to color the drum of its highest digit to indicate the total mileage is in excess of the capability of the odometer.

Electric Speedometers and Odometers

The electric speedometer and tachometer use a mechanically driven permanent magnet generator to supply power to a small electric motor. The electric motor then is used to rotate the input shaft of the speedometer or tachometer. The voltage from the generator will increase proportionally with speed, and speed will likewise increase proportionally with voltage enabling the gauges to indicate speed.

The signal generator for the speedometer is usually driven by the transmission output shaft through gears. The signal generator for the tachometer usually is driven by the distributor through a power takeoff on gasoline engines. When the tachometer is used with a diesel engine, a special power takeoff provision is made, usually on the camshaft drive.

Electronic Speedometers and Odometers

Electronic speedometers and Odometers are self-contained units that use an electric signal from the engine or transmission. They differ from the electric unit in that they use a generated signal as the driving force. The gauge is transistorized and will supply information through either a magnetic analog (dial) or light-emitting diode (LED) digital gauge display. The gauge unit derives its input signal in the following ways:

An electronic tachometer obtains a pulse signal from the ignition distributor, as it switches the coil on and off. The pulse speed at this point will change proportionally with engine speed. This is the most popular signal source for a tachometer that is used on a gasoline engine.

A tachometer that is used with a diesel engine uses the alternating current generated by the stator terminal of the alternator as a signal. The frequency of the ac current will change proportionally with engine speed.

An electronic speedometer derives its signal from a magnetic pickup coil that has its field interrupted by a rotating pole piece. The signal units operation is the same as the operation of the reluctor and pickup coil described earlier in this TRAMAN. The pickup coil is located strategically in the transmission case to interact with the reluctor teeth on the input shaft.

HORN

The horn currently used on automotive vehicles is the electric vibrating type. The electric vibrating horn system typically consists of a fuse, horn button switch, relay, horn assembly, and related wiring. When the operator presses the horn button, it closes the horn switch and activates the horn relay. This completes the circuit, and current is allowed through the relay circuit and to the horn.

Most horns have a diaphragm that vibrates by means of an electromagnetic. When the horn is energized, the electromagnet pulls on the horn diaphragm. This movement opens a set of contact points inside the horn. This action allows the diaphragm to flex back towards its normal position. This cycle is repeated rapidly. The vibrations of the diaphragm within the air column produce the note of the horn.

Tone and volume adjustments are made by loosening the adjusting locknut and turning the adjusting nut. This very sensitive adjustment controls the current consumed by the horn.

Increasing the current increases the volume. However, too much current will make the horn sputter and may lock the diaphragm.

When an electric horn will not produce sound, check the fuse, the connections, and test for voltage at the horn terminal. If the horn sounds continuously, a faulty horn switch is the most probable cause. A faulty horn relay is another cause of horn problems. The contacts inside the relay may be burned or stuck together.

WINDSHIELD WIPERS

The windshield wiper system is one of the most important safety factors on any piece of equipment. A typical electric windshield wiper system consists of a switch, motor assembly, wiper linkage and arms, and wiper blades. The description of the components is as follows:

The WINDSHIELD WIPER SWITCH is a multi position switch, which may contain a rheostat. Each switch position provides for different wiping speeds. The rheostat, if provided, operates the delay mode for a slow wiping action. This permits the operator to select a delayed wipe from every 3 to 20 seconds. A relay is frequently used to complete the circuit between the battery voltage and the wiper motor.

The WIPER MOTOR ASSEMBLY operates on one, two, or three speeds. The motor has a worm gear on the armature shaft that drives one or two gears, and, in turn, operates the linkage to the wiper arms. The motor is a small, shunt wound dc motor. Resistors are placed in the control circuit from the switch to reduce the current and provide different operating speeds.

The WIPER LINKAGE and ARMS transfer motion from the wiper motor transmission to the wiper blades. The rubber wiper blades fit on the wiper arms.

The WIPER BLADE is a flexible rubber squeegee-type device. It may be steel or plastic backed and is designed to maintain total contact with the windshield throughout the stroke. Wiper blades should be inspected periodically. If they are hardened, cut, or split, they are to be replaced.

When electrical problems occur in the windshield wiper system, use the service manual and its wiring diagram of the circuit. First check the fuses, electrical connections, and all grounds. Then proceed with checking the components.